I've known Jim Raley for many years and consider him a dear friend who always has a timely word from God to share with the body of Christ. His new book, *Hell's Spells*, is a must-read for anyone who wants to understand and overcome the ways that the enemy creeps into our homes and churches and tries to keep us from being everything God has created us to be.

—TOMMY BARNETT
SENIOR PASTOR OF PHOENIX FIRST ASSEMBLY
AND FOUNDER OF LOS ANGELES DREAM CENTER

Spiritual warfare is real, and if you're a Christian, you're in the battle whether you acknowledge it or not. Jim Raley's book, *Hell's Spells*, tells you how to identify and defeat some of the greatest weapons Satan uses in the lives of Christians and churches. I encourage you to read and apply this message to your life and watch it set you free.

—CHRISTINE CAINE
DIRECTOR, EQUIP AND EMPOWER MINISTRIES
FOUNDER, THE A21 CAMPAIGN

HELL'S SPELLS

JIM RALEY

CHARISMA
HOUSE

Most CHARISMA HOUSE BOOK GROUP products are available at special quantity discounts for bulk purchase for sales promotions, premiums, fund-raising, and educational needs. For details, write Charisma House Book Group, 600 Rinehart Road, Lake Mary, Florida 32746, or telephone (407) 333-0600.

HELL'S SPELLS by Jim Raley
Published by Charisma House
Charisma Media/Charisma House Book Group
600 Rinehart Road
Lake Mary, Florida 32746
www.charismahouse.com

Cover design by Justin Evans
Design Director: Bill Johnson

Visit the author's website at www.calvaryfl.com.

Library of Congress Cataloging-in-Publication Data:
An application to register this book for cataloging has been submitted to the Library of Congress.
International Standard Book Number: 978-1-61638-943-7
E-book ISBN: 978-1-61638-944-4

While the author has made every effort to provide accurate telephone numbers and Internet addresses at the time of publication, neither the publisher nor the author assumes any responsibility for errors or for changes that occur after publication.

First edition

12 13 14 15 16 — 9 8 7 6 5 4 3 2 1
Printed in the United States of America

To my children—Courtney, Channing, and Peyton—who give me the greatest honor imaginable every time they call me Dad, and to Dawn, the girl who stole my heart, my lasting love and my truest friend

CONTENTS

INTRODUCTION

IT IS CHALLENGING TO GET OUR MINDS AROUND THE POSSI-
bility that any Bible-believing Christian could contend with
any of hell's spells whatsoever. It seems in total contradiction and
contrast to all we have been taught and everything most of us have
been led to believe our entire Christian life. But shockingly and
sadly, much of the church has been charmed due to the power and
influence of hell's spells.

It is important to bring clarity to this matter at the very incep-
tion of this book. It's necessary to understand what I *am* and what I
am *not* referring to. When I talk about hell's spells, I am not saying
that we as a church are being threatened by witches, warlocks, or
soothsayers. Witches and warlocks have no power over the church
of the living God. But nevertheless, the church today has to contend greatly with hell's spells.

In the early church this reality was exposed and dealt with by
one of the greatest history makers who ever lived. Paul leveled an
intense accusation against the church in Galatia:

> O foolish Galatians! *Who has bewitched you* that you
> should not obey the truth, before whose eyes Jesus
> Christ was clearly portrayed among you as crucified?
> —GALATIANS 3:1, EMPHASIS ADDED

> Oh, foolish Galatians! What magician has hypnotized
> you and cast an evil spell upon you? For you used to see

the meaning of Jesus Christ's death as clearly as though
I had waved a placard before you with a picture on it of
Christ dying on the cross.

—GALATIANS 3:1, TLB

I wanted to show you two different translations to reiterate the fact that hell's spells can be present in the church. *Bewitched* is the word used in the New King James Version of the Bible, and it means the act of casting a spell, to charm, to fascinate, and to please to such degree as to take away the power of resistance. Much of the church has been fascinated and effectively charmed by the enemy, so much so that the power of its effectiveness has diminished greatly. This letter was written to all the churches throughout the region of Galatia over two thousand years ago, but it just as easily could have been addressed to yours and mine today.

My purpose for writing this book is to see those within the body of Christ empowered by a fresh awareness of the strategies of Satan. If we are to impose the power and plan of God on Planet Earth, we must expose the schemes of hell that would seek to sabotage our success. A church that does not resist the devil is no threat to him. Real resistance requires real revelation. You are the greatest threat to the satanic agenda when you are equipped with information that enables you to clearly identify and break the power of hell's spells over your life and circumstances.

This is a book that all of hell wishes you would not read. By the end of this journey you are going to be fully aware, fully awake, and fully cognizant of who you are in Christ and the power you have over the kingdom of darkness!

Welcome to the wake-up call.

Section I
PREPARING *for* BATTLE

Chapter 1

RISE *of the* HATER

W HATEVER YOU WANT TO CALL HIM—SATAN, LUCIFER, the big red fella, or just the plain ol' devil—understand this fact: he is real. He's not a little red cartoon character with pointed ears, a pointed tale, and a pitchfork. He is far more sinister and diabolical than that. Satan is alive and well, and he seeks to destroy you. In 1 Peter 5:8 the Bible says, "Your adversary the devil walks about like a roaring lion, seeking whom he may devour."

Even within Christian circles many today are choosing to ignore him and act as if he doesn't exist, and you know what? That's exactly what he desires! This is perhaps one of the most effective and deceptive spells hell has cast on humanity today. He knows the more covert he is, the more potent he can be. The late Keith Green had incredible insight when he penned some sobering words concerning Satan. The song "No One Believes in Me Anymore" is a narrative from the viewpoint of Satan concerning his own existence. He describes how easily he is gaining power by the hour because no one believes in him anymore. Satan is most effective when he is not acknowledged or believed in, and he knows it. Never forget; it's impossible to defeat an enemy that you refuse to admit exists.

One of the greatest tragedies of our day is that much of the church is filled with unbelieving believers, people who want only to believe the portions of the Bible that make them comfortable. Those who scoff at the existence of a literal devil surmise that to believe in such a being is illogical and unrealistic. But the question must be asked: Who's really being unrealistic? How else can we explain the moral and spiritual abyss that our society has plunged itself into? How can we justify the hundreds of millions of lives that have been wrecked, robbed, and ruined by war and famine? What about the Holocaust or the bombing of the World Trade Center? Every time a child is abused, a woman is raped, or someone is persecuted because of the color of his or her skin, it further reinforces the reality of an existing devil.

The ones who take exception to the belief in a real devil and his influence in the world would certainly then deny that he has any influence at all over their lives. The truth, however, is quite the contrary. Satan and his demons are consumed with influencing and affecting the individual lives of everyday people.

The longer I've lived, the more I've come to realize the devil has a scheme but God has a plan. Satan will do and is doing everything he can do to thwart the plan of God for your life. Satan doesn't just hate the world; he hates you. The hatred the devil operates is so volcanic and intense that it really defies logic. It's hard to imagine that there is such a being that has absolutely no redeeming qualities whatsoever. Satan is pure evil. He exists, and he is supremely dedicated to his unholy cause.

Understanding Your Adversary

I want to say this with great conviction and clarity: Satan is your adversary. He is more than just an enemy of God, the church, or the pastor. Satan is your personal adversary, and you will never have a greater foe than the devil. Peter called him "*your* adversary the devil." As this chapter unfolds, we will discover why this concept must be totally grasped and understood by every human being on Planet Earth.

Your destiny in this life and your eternal position in the life to come greatly hinge on your understanding of the devil. As you gain insight into Satan's schemes, you won't be filled with fear and dread; you will be filled with faith and victory! There is no need for you to fear the devil. The more you understand him, the less you will fear him! In fact, Satan's greatest fear as you read this book is that he will be found out to be the loser he really is.

Whatever God hates, Satan loves, and anything and anyone God loves, Satan hates. It only makes sense to question the origin of such a burning, boiling, unbridled hatred. The best way to understand Satan is to begin at his beginning, a time before he was even known as Satan, a time when he was called Lucifer, the Morning Star.

THE SAGA OF SATAN

In the Book of Ezekiel the spiritual fabric of time is torn back, and we catch a glimpse into eternity past. Lucifer started out incredibly blessed but became the most vile and corrupt creature in existence. Understanding the origin of Satan is an important piece of this puzzle, because this understanding will help explain how he has come to be who he is.

> You were the seal of perfection, full of wisdom and perfect in beauty. You were in Eden, the garden of God; every precious stone was your covering: the sardius, topaz, and diamond, beryl, onyx, and jasper, sapphire, turquoise, and emerald with gold. The workmanship of your timbrels and pipes was prepared for you on the day you were created.
>
> You were the anointed cherub who covers; I established you; you were on the holy mountain of God; you walked back and forth in the midst of fiery stones. You were perfect in your ways from the day you were created, till iniquity was found in you.
>
> By the abundance of your trading you became filled with violence within, and you sinned; therefore I cast you as a profane thing out of the mountain of God; and

3

> I destroyed you, O covering cherub, from the midst of
> the fiery stones.
>
> Your heart was lifted up because of your beauty; you
> corrupted your wisdom for the sake of your splendor; I
> cast you to the ground, I laid you before kings, that they
> might gaze at you.
>
> You defiled your sanctuaries by the multitude of your
> iniquities.
>
> —EZEKIEL 28:12–18

Wow! What a beginning! The Bible describes him as the model of perfection, full of wisdom and perfect in beauty. Without a doubt Lucifer had it going on. His wisdom and beauty were unmatched among God's created beings.

The Book of Hebrews tells us that our God is a consuming fire (Heb. 12:29). Satan walked among the fiery stones, which represent the presence of the Lord. In fact, he was called the guardian cherub. He walked among the coals of God's fiery presence. He hovered, covered, and kept company with God. His access to the heavenly Father was unhindered and unrestricted. This is unfathomable!

Lucifer was covered with jewels. Stunning and precious stones adorned him. His magnificent attractiveness was incredible and must have been a sight to behold. With stones fitted in gold and covering his entire body, he was a vision of awe and wonder. Can you imagine the dazzling prism of gorgeous Technicolor as he reflected the brilliant light and fire of God's holy presence? He was nothing less than the masterpiece of heaven.

But it didn't stop there. The Bible goes on to say that the workmanship of Lucifer's timbrels and pipes was prepared from the day he was created. Timbrels and pipes are musical terms. Lucifer was literally a musical instrument of worship himself. He didn't have to call for an instrument in order to worship God; he *was* an instrument. He was heaven's most perfect instrument of worship. In that time he brought the highest expression of praise to God in the universe.

Lucifer existed in an atmosphere of beauty and holiness. His purpose in the realm of glory had incredible significance. He was God's greatest creation and was obviously in charge of the worship in heaven. He was anointed by God and held a place of great influence and authority.

This provides amazing insight into why the enemy wars so vehemently against worship. Satan understands the presence of God and knows firsthand of the power of worship. He was granted access to the glory of God based on worship. And he knows that our ticket into God's glorious presence is worship as well. Satan comprehends that there is incredible power made available to worshippers. Have you ever noticed how much friction can come into a church over worship? The devil sows incredible division and confusion as styles and genres of music are often heatedly debated within Christian circles. The fact is, if people are quarreling and fretting over musical styles, they are not worshipping. Where people are not worshipping, they are denied access to God's presence. Satan knows that real change and total victory are found only in the presence of the Lord. He understands that when he keeps us from worship, he denies us our victory.

An Ugly Occurrence in a Beautiful Place

As beautiful and perfect as Lucifer was, he was a created being. There are many who might be thinking: Why in the world did God create the devil? He has caused so much pain, so much heartache, and so much trouble; why was the devil even created? That is actually a legitimate question with an easy answer. God did not create the devil. God created a perfect, moral, spiritual, and glorious being. The creator of the devil was the devil. When he allowed himself to fall prey to his own pride he created himself.

> Your heart was lifted up because of your beauty; you
> corrupted your wisdom for the sake of your splendor.
> —EZEKIEL 28:17

The day Lucifer lifted up himself in his heart was the beginning of the end for him. The Bible says that he corrupted his wisdom for the sake of his splendor. He knew what was right, he understood what was right, but his desire to be exalted corrupted his ability to even think logically. As wise as he was, he certainly understood that he was nothing without the Lord, yet he deceived his own self.

The Bible tells us that Satan is actually the father of all lies. That would make him the source and originator of every lie that has ever been told. As the originator of all lies, he had to tell the first one. Now here is a mind-boggling truth concerning Satan's lies. Satan's first lie was not to Eve, Adam, or even God. The first prey caught in the web of Satan's lies was Satan himself! The first victim of the devil was the devil. He had it all and he lost it all, because he became filled with pride and believed his own lie!

This is proven out in Scripture through the writings of a regal old prophet named Isaiah. This grand prophet of God had supernatural insight into the spirit realm. He was a spiritual time traveler. God revealed a prophetic preview of Christ the Messiah to him. Isaiah was shown specific events revolving around the birth, life, and crucifixion of Christ seven hundred years before they had even occurred.

But Isaiah also had insight into events that had taken place long before his time as well. God showed him a glimpse of an incredible day in heaven, the day that Lucifer fell.

> How you are fallen from heaven, O Lucifer, son of the
> morning! How you are cut down to the ground, you
> who weakened the nations! For you have said in your
> heart: "I will ascend into heaven, I will exalt my throne
> above the stars of God; I will also sit on the mount of
> the congregation on the farthest sides of the north; I will

ascend above the heights of the clouds, I will be like the
Most High."

—ISAIAH 14:12–14

The source and motivation behind Satan's lie was pride. Satan caught the dreaded "I will" disease. Five times in two verses he made the boastful statement "I will." And each of those statements was a lie. "I will ascend into heaven, I will exalt my throne above the stars of God, I will sit on the mount of the congregation on the farthest sides of the north, I will ascend above the clouds, *I will be like the Most High*." He knew better, but blinded by his pride, he believed his own lies.

Even today when men and women are filled with pride, right thinking goes out the window. We deceive ourselves into thinking that we can do whatever we want to do. We convince ourselves we can have impure sexual relationships, participate in sinful acts, and do as we please—and it doesn't matter. We become blinded by our own pride, and like the father of lies we deceive our own selves. And just as the greatest victim of Satan's lies was Satan, the greatest victim of our lies is ourselves.

Pride on Satan's part was absolutely irrational; everything he had was given to him. The jewels were incredibly gorgeous, but they only reflected the light of God's presence and glory. No jewel or precious stone reflects its own light, because it has no light of its own. If you put a beautiful diamond in a dark room, no one will see it; it is only when it reflects a source of light that it is even noticeable. A jewel is nothing without the light, and Lucifer was nothing without the light of God.

Lucifer's beauty was nonexistent outside the presence of God. It was God who had made him, and only God could make him shine. It's the same with us, isn't it? We are our most lovely when the presence of the Lord shines brightly through our lives. We were created by God and for God, just as Lucifer was. The apex of Lucifer's life was when he was giving glory to God and not himself. He was at his most beautiful and productive as he was willing to remain faithful to the purpose God created him for.

> Thou art worthy, O Lord, to receive glory and honour and power: for thou hast created all things, and for thy pleasure they are and were created.
> —REVELATION 4:11, KJV

God created everything and everyone for His pleasure. In our modern Western society we understand pleasure in a one-dimensional facet. Pleasure in our world today means to be totally self-indulgent and self-gratifying. The Greek overtones of this word in the original language of the New Testament are very different. The English word translated *pleasure* is actually the Greek word *thelema*. *Thelema* in this context means will, choice, desire, and purpose. This is very significant because it further reinforces the fact again that we were created by God and for God. He has specific desires and purposes for everyone He created, and we exist to fulfill them. We live at and for His pleasure.

Just as it happened with Lucifer, when our life's focus shifts from God's pleasure to ours, ugly things begin to happen. Lucifer was in that place of perfect peace, love, and obedience. He was functioning at the very summit of his purpose, and it was a beautiful place. The prophet of God said he was perfect in his ways from the day he was created until iniquity (sin) was found in him. When that day occurred, everything that was beautiful on the outside of Lucifer was corrupted by what went on inside him. Corruption and sin on the inside always lead to trouble and trial on the outside.

Something that started out so beautiful has morphed into all the ugly that is seen in Satan today. Why? Because Lucifer allowed sin to enter his heart and sin makes everything ugly. Sin can make a beautiful marriage an ugly one. Sin will transform a magnificent promising life into an ugly, broken, and fractured existence. Sin makes everything ugly.

SATAN'S SELF-DESTRUCTION

Satan had the absolute dream job. He gave glory to God. But somewhere along the line he lost sight of the fact that he was made to worship and not for worship. Instead of giving God glory and worship, he sought to receive it, and no one, and I mean no one, can handle worship except for God. There is not a single created being that can handle being worshipped. Those who receive worship unto themselves wind up doing just what Satan did, and that's self-destructing.

We have all witnessed many people over the years who have self-destructed when they've attempted to receive worship unto themselves. Celebrities, rock stars, and even those who've gained notoriety and success in Christian circles have imploded when they have allowed themselves to be worshipped. The obvious and undeniable truth is this: people are not made for worship. No matter how gifted, charismatic, persuasive, or motivational a person may be, he or she is not built to handle worship; only God is. History reinforces this fact as we look at the ever-growing list of the crumbled lives of those who became convinced that they were "worship worthy." They've overdosed on drugs, committed suicide, or killed their own mighty ministries and dreams because they allowed themselves to be worshipped.

The thing about man-related worship is this: being worshipped will change a man. I've watched good people become manipulative, self-seeking, self-motivated, and self-exalting. They started off right, but as they began to personally crave and desire worship, they became lovers of themselves and users of God's precious people. Just like Satan's desire to be worshipped changed him from a being of honor to one of dishonor, it has the very same effect on us.

Worship of a man will change a man. But thankfully and gloriously worship does not change God, because He never changes! Worship does not change God; on the contrary, worship reveals Him. The more we worship God, the greater access we have to Him.

With that greater access we are granted the incalculable blessing of knowing more about Him. My worship reveals more about His love, His healing power, His provision, and His forgiving nature. He is made known and revealed in times of worship, and I am truly grateful. He remains unchanged as I worship Him, but there is a change that takes place, and it's the greatest change of all! The change that takes place is in me! True worship doesn't change God; it changes us! Time in the presence of the Lord will make us more loving, more giving, more long-suffering, more victorious, and just plain better.

> Worship does not change God; on the contrary, worship reveals Him.

When Satan was filled with pride, he self-destructed. Pride is a terrible thing; it changed an angel into a devil. And if pride can do that to Lucifer, what can it do to us?

THE RISE OF THE HATER

Pride and sin created and manifested Satan, but the question still must be answered: Why are we so loathed and abhorred by him? What gave rise to our hater, and why is his hatred so incessant and unrelenting as it relates to humanity? There are three main reasons behind Satan's hatred, and I want to reveal them to you personally. These explanations will help you understand why Satan hates you and why he has focused his hatred so intensely on you. Prepare yourself, because as you continue to read, you will begin to understand why Satan is your personal adversary.

Satan hates you because every time he sees you, he sees God.

Now I am certainly not saying that we are God, but we are a reflection of Him. We are made in the image of our Creator.

God said, "Let Us make man in Our image, according
to Our likeness."
—Genesis 1:26

There is something very powerful and precious about human
life. Satan gets it even if we don't. He fully comprehends that there
is nothing on Planet Earth more valuable or sacred than a human
being made in God's own image.

Most of us will call an exterminator and kill every bug in the
house without a second thought! We will sit down and have a delicious meal consisting of some kind of meat taken from a slain
animal and then talk about how delicious it was. But if we were to
cause harm or death to a fellow human being, the guilt and pain of
that act would be almost impossible to bear.

What is it about human life that is so incredibly precious? What
makes a person's life so valuable that medical professionals will fight
to keep a newborn baby alive or spend millions of dollars treating a
disease to save even one individual? Why are we set apart and different from every other living thing in the universe?

It all comes down to being made in the image of God. In
studying the process of creation, we find that the creation of man is
different from every other part of creation. Every act of creation in
Genesis 1 is impersonal all the way up until verse 26. Before verse
26 we read phrases such as, "Let there be…" Prior to the creation
of man every other creature is described as being created according
to its kind. God spoke and made a zebra to look like a zebra, a butterfly to look like a butterfly, and a turtle to look like a turtle. He
did this through the whole of the animal kingdom. There was no
template for these animals; each one was created through the bril-
liance and knowledge of God, according to their kind.

However, in verse 26 we see a radical shift. God moves from,
"Let there be…" to "Let Us make." And God doesn't stop with just
the personal statement "Let Us make man"; He adds to it three
powerful words: "in Our image"! Man's image and likeness are not

simply of himself. Man's image and likeness come from God. Satan does not hate the rest of creation the way he hates you, and there is a powerful reason why. The rest of creation does not remind him of God, but you do!

Satan hates you because you are connected to God in a way that the rest of creation will never be, including him. As great, powerful, and wonderful as Lucifer was in heaven, we are never led to believe that he was made in the image of God. You are, and for that reason he hates you.

Satan hates you because you have stolen his job, and you're better at it than he was!

Remember now, Satan was the worship leader in heaven. The worship he brought to God was the most beautiful thing in all the cosmos. There was nothing in the universe at that time that compared to the incredible expression of praise and glory that Lucifer presented to God. But he lost his way, and when he lost his way, he lost his job.

He had been a literal instrument of glory to the Lord. His exquisite loveliness was a breathtaking spectacle, as the jewels that covered him reflected the shimmering light of God's powerful presence. He was awesome, but he was not irreplaceable. No matter how great or gifted we think we are, we are not irreplaceable either.

There is now a new reflection of God's light present today. It's not just another angel or heavenly being. The new reflection of God's light and glory is you and me. It's His children who have been redeemed by the power of the cross of Jesus Christ. We, not Lucifer, are the light bearers of the universe now. In Matthew 5:14 Jesus actually identifies us as the light of the world. I love the way *The Message* Bible interprets this passage of Scripture:

> Here's another way to put it: You're here to be light, bringing out the God-colors in the world. God is not a secret to be kept. We're going public with this, as public

> as a city on a hill. If I make you light-bearers, you don't
> think I'm going to hide you under a bucket, do you? I'm
> putting you on a light stand. Now that I've put you there
> on a hilltop, on a light stand—shine!
> —MATTHEW 5:14–15, THE MESSAGE

We, not Lucifer, are now the reflection of God's light. He got fired, FOR REAL, and we took his job! The beautiful jewels that reflected the glory of God have been stripped from Lucifer, and we don't find them again in the Bible until the Book of Revelation. The next time we read of them, the saints of God are covered with these same jewels in the heavenlies, and you know what they are doing? They are worshipping God!

We took Lucifer's job, and we are better at it than he ever was. Our worship is sweeter, our worship is more beautiful, and here's the reason why.

> And they sang a new song, saying: "You are worthy to
> take the scroll, and to open its seals; for You were slain,
> and have redeemed us to God by Your blood out of every
> tribe and tongue and people and nation, and have made
> us kings and priests to our God; and we shall reign on
> the earth."
> —REVELATION 5:9–10

Our song is the loveliest song in the entire universe because it's the song of the redeemed! We have a new song that even the angels can't sing! It is perpetually on heaven's hit list and will be so through the ages! We have been rescued and redeemed through the power of the blood of Jesus. God's "Amazing Grace" is the song and the source of the most beautiful worship ever offered before the throne. Satan knows it, and Satan hates it.

Satan hates your worship because every time you worship God, you remind him of what he used to be and will never be again. And not only that, but also you sing a song unto the Lord that he has never and will never sing! He hates your song, so sing it loud!

There is nothing worse than a Christian without a song. Never let the devil steal your song. Don't give him the power to rob you of your worship. I believe that worship is one of the most effective tools of spiritual warfare that you possess. If you really want to cause the devil pain and thwart his scheme for your life, just make up your mind to become a worshipper, and then...sing your song!

It's your song of gratitude, but in many ways, it's heaven's best revenge!

Satan hates you so much because God loves you so much.

God loves you so much. Stop for just one moment and let that peace-bringing, hope-giving statement sink into every fiber in your being. God. Loves. You. So. Much. In fact, why not make that statement personal? Declare this very moment, "God loves me so much!"

> For God *so* loved the world...
> —JOHN 3:16, EMPHASIS ADDED

God doesn't just love the world; He *so* loves the world. God loves the world, God loves nations, but never forget, God loves the one. Understand this fact: He loves you personally. He loves you with a love that is colossal, immeasurable, and unearnable. He loves you through your struggles, your issues, and far beyond your failures. Your ups and your downs change nothing about God's love for you. His love is so incredible and full throttle that there is not one thing you can do that will make Him love you any more or any less. He loves you to the ultimate degree and to the highest level. He loves you *so* much. Even those days when you feel there is *no* love, just remember, you are *so* loved.

Satan's hate is one of the most powerful forces in the universe, but it's not the most powerful force.

The only thing greater than Satan's hate is God's love.

Satan understands the magnitude of God's love for you, and there is no way to describe how much Satan hates God. His ultimate desire is to wound the heart of God. How do you think he would best go about hurting the heart of God? By attacking those God so loves. He knows the best way to cause God pain is to cause you pain. He knows when he breaks your heart, he is actually breaking God's heart. If you have children, you understand this concept; the greatest harm and pain someone can bring into your life is for them to hurt your children. It is an incredible thing when we realize that we are actually more than just God's creation; we are His children.

> What marvelous love the Father has extended to us! Just look at it—we're called children of God! That's who we really are.
> —1 JOHN 3:1, THE MESSAGE

We weep over nothing or anyone as we do our children, and we really are God's children. It seems a difficult and hard concept to grasp, but God loves us, so He will weep over us. Yes, even the Lord of all will weep over those whom He so loves.

> Now as He drew near, he saw the city and wept over it.
> —LUKE 19:41

Can you imagine? We catch a glimpse of God's heart through this act of Christ while on the earth. Jesus, God the Son, weeps over the people He loves. We serve a heavenly Father who is not calloused, cold, or indifferent toward us. He is not distracted and disconnected from His children, but He loves us all with great passion and emotion. This gives us real clarity into understanding the ultimate source of Satan's immense antagonism toward us. The ultimate source of Satan's great hate for you is simply this: God's great love for you. This is the fuel that feeds the fiery hatred of the devil like nothing else. It is God's matchless love that gives rise to Satan's monstrous hate.

If we are not careful, Satan's hate can overwhelm us. If that happens, we fall into Satan's trap. We will begin to worry about the effectiveness and strength of Satan's hate rather than the mighty force of God's love. We will walk in fear, doubt, and worry, concerned about every attack of the enemy. But don't, because although Satan's hate is powerful, it is not unstoppable. The love of God will stop Satan's hate dead in its tracks every time. Consistently remind yourself of this: there is no greater power in the universe than the love of God. The apostle Paul had a grasp on this when he penned these incredible words in a letter to the Christians in Rome.

> So, what do you think? With God on our side like this, how can we lose? If God didn't hesitate to put everything on the line for us, embracing our condition and exposing himself to the worst by sending his own Son, is there anything else he wouldn't gladly and freely do for us? And who would dare tangle with God by messing with one of God's chosen? Who would dare even to point a finger? The One who died for us—who was raised to life for us!—is in the presence of God at this very moment sticking up for us. Do you think anyone is going to be able to drive a wedge between us and Christ's love for us? There is no way! Not trouble, not hard times, not hatred, not hunger, not homelessness, not bullying threats, not backstabbing, not even the worst sins listed in Scripture: They kill us in cold blood because they hate you. We're sitting ducks; they pick us off one by one. None of this fazes us because Jesus loves us. I'm absolutely convinced that nothing—nothing living or dead, angelic or demonic, today or tomorrow, high or low, thinkable or unthinkable—absolutely nothing can

get between us and God's love because of the way that
Jesus our Master has embraced us.

—ROMANS 8:31–39, THE MESSAGE

Wow! With that kind of promise from the Word of God it would
be an incredible tragedy to sit around and worry about a hater
named Satan! Don't waste your days focused on Satan's hate, but
spend your days feasting on God's love! God loves you personally,
and there's not one thing the devil can do about it—and by the way,
you can't either!

Chapter 2

KNOW *Your* FOE

O NE OF THE MOST MISUNDERSTOOD SUBJECTS IN THE whole of Christian theology and teaching is the subject of spiritual warfare. Oftentimes when topics like this are discussed, well, it can have a tendency to get a little weird. People can get strange, leaders can get strange, and church gatherings can get strange. So then, many times, rather than taking these important topics head-on, Bible preachers and teachers will avoid them all together. When this occurs, we do great harm to those within the body of Christ who desperately need to be empowered, impacted, and prepared for spiritual battle. Hell's spells are in full affect when the church ignores the reality of spiritual warfare. We will never win a war we refuse to acknowledge.

There is no need to sensationalize spiritual warfare, because it's already sensational! The fact that there is a world that exists beyond this world is sensational, don't you think? A world in the spirit realm that is every bit as real as the world you and I live in and understand right now? A world filled with angels, demons, a devil, and an almighty God? That's amazing!

What I have often seen in many Christian circles, however, are manipulations and misunderstandings as it relates to this subject. I have witnessed this teaching sensationalized in such a way as to provoke public interest and excitement *at the expense of biblical accuracy.* All teaching and revelation on this subject must rest on the firm foundation of biblical truth. Anything else is inaccurate and will lead us to trouble and often to fear. And as born-again believers, we have nothing to fear! The only way for a believer to lose in spiritual warfare is to refuse to fight. And when you finally make up your mind to fight, it's of the utmost importance to know your foe.

The first key to victory in spiritual warfare is this: you must believe in the spirit realm. You must believe that this realm is real and tangible. The spirit realm is not some made-up fairy tale that lives only in the minds of children and the superstitious, but it is real. In other words, you must believe that what you see isn't all there is. You must believe and acknowledge that there is more.

> The only way for a believer to lose in spiritual warfare is to refuse to fight.

Spiritual warfare is something that takes place every day. It is going on twenty-four hours a day, and it is happening whether we realize it or not. Just because we ignore something doesn't mean it doesn't exist. Many people suffer from the sickness of "ostrichitus." They think if they act like an ostrich about things like spiritual warfare, then it's not happening. They may stick their head in the sand and ignore it, but it's still occurring! Are you suffering from ostrichitus? Well, if you are, then I have good news for you: this book is the cure for ostrichitus as it relates to spiritual warfare.

One of the greatest and most respected voices in modern Christianity believes in spiritual warfare. Billy Graham explains the reality of spiritual warfare in his book *Angels*. He describes this spiritual struggle as a war that began in the heart of Lucifer himself.[1]

There is incredible spiritual warfare that takes place with unremitting relentlessness. Wherever God is at work, satanic forces are as well. The powers of hell seek to sabotage and destroy God's plan and agenda for every man, woman, boy, and girl on Planet Earth. Since his fall from heaven Lucifer has not let up. He is the master of deceit, and he and his demonic forces do all they can to enforce satanic rule.

The devil is serious about spiritual warfare, and we must be as well. Satan is more desperate, determined, and fiercer than he has ever been. As we race toward the end of the age, he sees and knows firsthand the victory of the cross of Jesus Christ. There must be no doubt, this is war.

> …be vigilant; because your adversary the devil…
> —1 PETER 5:8

Adversary is a warrior's term. Satan is desperately fighting to destroy you, your destiny, your purpose, and your family. But do not be overcome or dismayed. If you are a believer in Jesus, you are a winner!

You may be thinking, "Thank you for telling me this, because I surely don't feel like a winner!" It's kind of like the boxer who was fighting a powerful opponent. He was getting beaten up pretty badly. His nose was bloody and broken, his lips were wounded and bleeding, and his eye was swollen shut. The bell rang, and he went to his corner and his trainer said, "You're doing great; he's not even laying a hand on you!" The struggling boxer looked at his trainer out of his one good eye and replied, "Well, then, you better keep your eye on that referee, because somebody in there is about to beat me to death!" We have all been in that place, haven't we? There have been times when we felt like we were losing horribly in our spiritual fight. You may be in that situation right now, but I want to encourage you. Your outcome is already in place. As you trust in the Lord, you will win—and you are winning!

Before we can grasp what spiritual warfare is, we must acknowledge what it is not. Unfortunately in much of the church realm today, we have not gotten a clear picture of spiritual warfare. Let me make something very clear: spiritual warfare is not shouting, screaming, or hollering. It's not raising the volume of your voice and threatening the devil. If you really have power, you can whisper and demons will tremble. I am not saying that there is one thing wrong with passion and emotion, but none of this is spiritual warfare.

> ...while we do not look at the things which are seen, but at the things which are not seen. For the things which are seen are temporary, but the things which are not seen are eternal.
>
> —2 CORINTHIANS 4:18

Paul declares here that there is a world that is not seen. This is a supernatural world, and in this unseen world is where spiritual warfare occurs. From the very beginning of time there has been a blurry line between the natural world and the spiritual world. At the dawn of creation, when Adam and Eve arrived in the Garden of Eden, Satan did too, and spiritual warfare began.

This struggle is called war because Satan and all of hell are in total rebellion to God. Spiritual warfare can manifest in many different ways. When we are tempted to participate in sin and unrighteous behavior, the fight is on. It occurs when we are wounded, hurt, or disappointed by those we love or have confidence in. It's a spiritual fight not to become bitter, angry, and unforgiving. The enemy will orchestrate situations that are engineered to defeat us, and it can become a struggle to remain victorious, joyful, and even saved!

Spiritual warfare can take place anywhere—at home, at work, and even at church! Never forget; the devil has been known to go to church. Now it's important that you understand this truth: there is great spiritual warfare occurring at this very moment. You might be wondering if God is worried, and that answer would be a resounding no. God is in total control and is in no danger from Satan at all.

We are engaged in war, the stakes are enormous, and our enemy is Satan.

Our enemy is God's enemy, and that enemy is Satan. In order for you to overcome an enemy, it is of utmost importance to know your foe. When you know your foe, you are on the path to certain victory.

Satan is not a wicked god who is the evil version of Jehovah God. He wants you to think he is, but don't give him that kind of credit. He is not God at all; he is a fallen angel. Satan is a created being. God, on the other hand, was never created; He is Creator. He has always been and will always be. He is all powerful and has no limitations. That's one of the things that make Him God. In contrast, Satan is not all powerful, and he has limitations. There is tremendous advantage gained by the believer who recognizes and exploits the weaknesses of the devil.

Be confident and courageous as you gain understanding; all of heaven is on your side! Let's take a look at some of the weaknesses of the devil.

SATAN IS LIMITED BY TIME

The clock is ticking on the devil, and his time is almost up.

> When He had come to the other side, to the country of the Gergesenes, there met Him two demon-possessed men, coming out of the tombs, exceedingly fierce, so that no one could pass that way. And suddenly they cried out, saying, "What have we to do with You, Jesus, You Son of God? Have You come here to torment us before the time?"
>
> —MATTHEW 8:28–29

This is a powerful example, because even though the devil and demons might not understand exactly when their time is up, even in the days of Christ they understood that their time would run out.

It doesn't take much of a Bible scholar to recognize that we are speeding quickly toward the end of this age. There is a time limit on satanic rebellion; he knows this, and obviously his time is running out. Pay close attention to how the demons responded to Jesus. They asked the Lord, "Why have you come to torment us before *the* time?" The original Greek word for "time" in this text is the word *kairos*. It means a set time, a predetermined time, or an allotted amount of time. This is why the demons asked the Lord, "Why have You come to torment us before *the* time?" They knew they had some time left, that their allotted amount of time had not run out yet.

Even in your life Satan cannot attack you forever. As you walk in faith, remember these powerful words:

> Weeping may endure for a night, but joy comes in the morning.
> —PSALM 30:5

This is good news! You will win if you don't give in. Joy will come. The devil's attack against your life has a *kairos* attached to it. It will not last forever. Don't quit fighting. Satan cannot attack you always. Even during difficult seasons of life, when times are hard and it seems like attacks are coming from every side, be strong in Jesus's name!

> Resist the devil and he will flee from you.
> —JAMES 4:7

Instead of hanging your head and giving up, rise up in faith, resist the devil, and remind him of this fact: "Satan, your time is running out!"

Satan is limited by time, but God *is* time. God doesn't move in time; time moves in God. Jesus introduced Himself to John the revelator as the *Alpha* (Greek alphabet first letter) and *Omega* (Greek alphabet last letter). Jesus, God the Son, was declaring to John, "I am the A, and I am the Z." God is the beginning and God is the end, and He is everything in between! He was letting John know in essence, "I have no beginning, and I have no ending." Wherever you were, God is. Wherever you are, God is there. Wherever you're going in your tomorrows, God is already there because God is not held in place by time; time is held in place by God. So let me reinforce this truth: Satan is limited in time, but God is time. This means as long as you have God, you have time!

SATAN IS LIMITED IN POWER

It is foolish to view Satan as all powerful because only God is all-powerful. In fact, power belongs exclusively to God. When God kicked Satan out of heaven, He certainly didn't release him with unlimited power. God is using Satan even now to reveal the heart of humanity by separating the just from the unjust. But Satan doesn't have any real power over God, or even us!

> Then I saw an angel coming down from heaven, having the key to the bottomless pit and a great chain in his hand. He laid hold of the dragon, that serpent of old, who is the Devil and Satan, and bound him for a thousand years.
> —REVELATION 20:1–2

This is an amazing passage of Scripture. After the Great Tribulation *one* angel binds up the devil and casts him into the pit. Not Jesus, not an army of angels, not even an archangel like Michael or Gabriel; it just takes one ordinary angel.

Why do we worry so much about the devil? He does not have the power to defeat even one angel. And the angels of the Lord are on your side!

> For he will order his angels to protect you wherever you
> go. They will hold you up with their hands so you won't
> even hurt your foot on a stone.
>
> —Psalm 91:11–12, nlt

Satan has limited power, but not only that; Satan has boundaries.

Satan Has Boundaries

He cannot do all that he would like to do, because he is hindered by boundaries. If he could do whatever he wanted to do to us, none of us would be alive right now. He has boundaries. This is a very important concept to grasp. As a spiritual being, Satan does not have the power to harm you, a physical being. *Satan does not have the power to physically touch you, nor can he force you to do anything.*

It kind of shoots in the foot the adage that says, "The devil made me do it." The devil has no power to make a man or woman do anything they don't agree to do. The only real power Satan has over our lives is the power we yield to him.

Though Satan cannot touch you physically or force you to do anything, this does not discount the power he does have. We can look at the condition of our world and fully comprehend that he does have tremendous power. The power Satan wields he wields brilliantly. The main source of his power is revealed in Paul's writing to the early church in Ephesus.

> Put on the whole armor of God, that you may be able
> to stand against the *wiles* of the devil. For we do not
> wrestle against flesh and blood, but against principali-
> ties, against powers, against the rulers of the darkness
> of this age, against spiritual hosts of wickedness in the
> heavenly places.
>
> —Ephesians 6:11–12, emphasis added

The word Paul uses to describe Satan's weapons is the word *wiles*. In this context *wiles* is defined as cunning arts, trickery, and deceit. Now I want you to think about that. This word does not represent a single natural weapon. There is not one thing about the word *wiles* that even gives a hint that Satan has any power to physically touch you. This is why Paul said, "We do not wrestle against flesh and blood." Satan uses trickery and deceit to do his damage! His ultimate desire is to take your life and destiny captive, and he never has to touch you to do it!

MIND GAMES

Satan is the master of the mind game. He is the ultimate schemer! And it is imperative that believers are aware of his tactics in order to be able to wage effective spiritual warfare.

> …so that Satan will not outsmart us. For we are familiar with his evil *schemes*.
> —2 CORINTHIANS 2:11, NLT, EMPHASIS ADDED

Paul understood Satan's tactics. The word *schemes* here in this verse means mental perceptions and thoughts—in other words, mind games. Many are outsmarted by the devil because of his incredible ability to play mind games. The truth is, he operates so strongly in this capacity that it is impossible for us to beat him alone. If we try to fight the devil alone, we are as good as defeated.

Remember, we cannot fight Satan with natural weapons. This is why the Bible says we don't wrestle against flesh and blood. Spiritual warfare is a different kind of fight with a different kind of foe. When we gain insight into this, we are on the path to certain victory.

Read this next verse very slowly, because contained in these fifteen words is the most powerful secret to achieving success and defeating the devil.

> Finally, my brethren, be strong in the Lord and in the
> power of His might.
> —EPHESIANS 6:10

This is an empowering and liberating scripture that deserves a closer look! Often we read a text like this and rush over missing the true promise that is contained within it. Let's break this scripture down and dissect it.

Finally

The first word we read in this scripture is the word *finally*. "Finally" is the Greek word *loipon*, and it means "hereafter, for the future, or from this point on." Now connect that word to the next part of this scripture.

Be strong in the Lord and in the power of His might

Paul was declaring, "Finally, hereafter, for the future, and from this point on, be strong in the Lord and in the power of His might." This lets us know that whatever strength we were convinced we had before would not be adequate for this fight.

When we think we have the power to fight the devil on our own, we are sadly mistaken. We cannot buy our victory over Satan, so our wealth is irrelevant in this fight. Our talent, gifting, skills, and connections will be inadequate for victory over this foe, and *finally* we need to realize it.

None of your abilities are sufficient in winning the fight against the devil. So finally, hereafter, and from this point forward, be strong in the Lord and in the power of His might. Spiritual warfare is never waged in your power and in your might but in God's. There is great breakthrough and victory in arriving at your "finally." Maybe you feel like you've been taking a pretty good beating, or you just can't seem to get real victory, but as you are reading this, the Spirit of the Lord is bringing you to your "finally!"

The strength that enables us to overcome is strength we receive from the Lord and not strength we possess on our own. Power belongs to God, and in our most intense struggles we will only know victory through and by His mighty strength.

Satan never has been and never will be defeated, detoured, or made afraid because of our power. The only power Satan fears is the power of God, and the only name that makes him tremble is the name of Jesus. Satan fears us only when we are depending on the Lord. When we try to operate in our own strength, that is when we get into trouble.

> Therefore let him who thinks he stands take heed lest he fall.
> —1 CORINTHIANS 10:12

Even in those times when we think we have it all figured out and under control, we need to take heed. Our strength can only be counted on when opposition is weak and temptations are small. To quote my old southern preacher granddad, "Any demon you can handle without the power of God ain't much of a demon!" When you get in a real fight with a real devil, you need the real power of a real God!

PLAYTIME IS OVER!

Satan loves to play mind games, but there is far too much at stake for us to be playing games with the enemy. Playtime is over! Since Satan cannot physically touch you, he wars against your mind. The power Satan uses is the power to influence us to act in opposition to God's Word. He will feed our minds with unholy and sinful thoughts. He will cause us to become fearful, doubtful, and prideful.

Satan will use situations, circumstances, and life experiences in order to fill our lives with sin, chaos, and trouble. Remember, he can't touch a physical being, because he is a spiritual being. He uses *wiles*. He deceives, tricks, and misleads.

Now get ready, because we are jumping into the deep end of the pool! Satan does not harm a man; he deceives a man, and then that man harms himself and others. The only control Satan has over us is the control that we yield to him. He only operates in the control we surrender to him.

We must not toy with the devil; we must resist him and his deceitful ways.

JOB AND JUDAS

The Bible gives us two amazing examples of men the enemy came against in a great way. When we compare these two and how each responded differently to changing circumstances, we can learn some powerful lessons.

Let's start with Job. Job had it going on. In fact, he is described as a man whom God had hedged about. He was blessed beyond imagination in every area of his life. Satan was convinced that if there was a shift in Job's circumstances, Job would surely deny God and give up.

God allowed Job to be tested through his circumstances. When Job had everything stripped away from him, to the shock and dismay of the devil he remained faithful to the Lord. Job proved that he loved God completely and totally, regardless of his circumstances. Job had a genuine relationship with God that was not hinging on the blessings he had received from the Lord. He had faith, trust, and love for God that remained strong even through hard situations.

If our love for God only remains true when our situations are perfect, Satan will defeat us. Satan thought for sure Job would be defeated when he lost the things he held dear. Satan failed to understand that Job was not focused on things; he was focused on God! Never allow the things that God gives you to become more important than the God who gave them to you.

The devil tried to play mind games with Job and lost horribly!

Now let's look at the life of Judas. He walked with Jesus on a personal level. He was intimately acquainted with the Lord and witnessed His miracle-working power firsthand. He was up close and personal when Jesus healed the sick, fed the hungry, and walked on water. With his own eyes he saw Jesus call Lazarus out of the tomb and open blind eyes. He saw all this, but still he lost his way.

The problem with Judas was this: he had his own personal agenda. He wanted Jesus to set up an earthly kingdom because he wanted a position for himself within that kingdom. When Judas discovered that Jesus had another agenda, the enemy tempted Judas, and he fell. Can't you hear the thoughts and suggestions the devil interjected into the mind of Judas? "Jesus is not who you thought He was. He's not going to move in the way you thought He was going to. He's not going to become what you desired. You have wasted your time following Him. You need to get what you deserve." And for thirty pieces of silver, he betrayed the King of all kings!

In that act of betrayal the root of Satan's deception is revealed. Satan convinced Judas to put his trust in things, and when Judas did, he was unfulfilled. He wound up committing suicide. Satan exploited and revealed a sad truth and weakness about Judas. *Judas was never in love with Jesus; he was only in love with what he thought Jesus could give him.* I have an important word for you: *stay in love with Jesus!*

Stay in love with Jesus, and it really won't matter what the enemy throws against you during the hard times. There are seasons when God will allow you to face hard times, but He will use those very situations to draw you closer to Him! Satan will use your circumstances, but so will God! Whether it be a financial attack, sickness, or people issues, God can and will use it. When you come through hard times, you actually have a greater love for the Lord! You have more faith, peace, power, and favor.

If the devil had any sense, he would leave you alone!

Satan wants to use your circumstances to cause you to doubt, fear, give up, and quit. He will try to convince you to just give up in your walk with God because it's just not worth it. But God will use your toughest times to reveal Himself to you in the biggest ways.

Andraé Crouch sang a song years ago. I remember it as a little boy. I can hear my sister playing the piano and my family singing it even now all these years later. The name of the song was "Through It All." In this song Crouch thanks God for the valleys, storms, and trials of his life. He does this because through it all—through his hardest times—he learned to trust in Jesus and rely on His Word.

Wow! That's powerful stuff right there! God is using your hardest times to reveal Himself to you. If you're coming through some trouble right now, be encouraged! You're going to make it, and when you come out on the other side, you'll know God in a greater way!

My Fiercest Foe

As you read this, you're probably thinking, "Well, I know who my fiercest foe is; it's the devil." And respectfully, that would be a 100 percent wrong answer. The most intense weapon Satan uses against us is our own selfish desires. I have come to understand a true fact in my own life: the most effective weapon Satan uses against me is me! I am my own fiercest foe. He uses my own selfish desires and my own bad attitudes and weaknesses against me.

Our own selfish desires can get us into so much trouble! This is why we must keep our desires submitted to Jesus. Satan wants our desires to make our decisions. And we are in serious trouble when we allow our desires to make our decisions. We must ask ourselves an honest question. Are we Spirit led or desire driven? This is important when we realize that Satan cannot make us do anything we don't desire to do. He will use our own desires to cause us to fall into sin.

When we submit our desires to the devil, he becomes the puppet master of our lives. Whoever controls your desires controls you. This is why you must resist the devil. There are actually three steps to overcoming the devil as it relates to his influence over your life and desires.

1. Know what is right.

The way we find out what is right is through receiving direction from God's Word. The Bible gives us clear and concise instructions on how to live our lives. We gain understanding through God's Word, and by the power of the Holy Spirit we know what is right.

The Word of God is the final authority on right and wrong behavior. We often give that power to religion, people, society, and even ourselves. All these sources are inept and inadequate. Even if we feel like something is right or wrong on a personal level, if it contradicts the Word of God, then it's wrong.

> There is a way that seems right to a man, but in the end
> it leads to death.
> —PROVERBS 16:25, NIV

That means it can feel right and still be wrong. Satan is banking on the fact that we will be controlled by our feelings and will ignore the Word of the Lord.

In much of our society truth has become viewed as relevant. Relevant truth says this: truth adjusts and changes according to our circumstances. Truth is whatever we desire it to be or need it to be according to the moment we are living in. But that is wrong. Relevant truth is not really truth at all, because truth doesn't change.

The Bible is absolute truth, and absolute truth is changeless. The wrongs and rights of the Bible remain intact from generation to generation. What was right in God's Word yesterday is still right in God's Word today; what was wrong in God's Word yesterday is still wrong today. Society changes, religion changes, and people change, but the Word of God remains true.

The key to knowing what is right is found in knowing God's Word.

2. Desire what is right.

It is a beautiful thing when we begin to desire what is right. The devil loses tremendous influence over our lives when our desire for what's right takes preeminence in our day-to-day living. We are not saved or unsaved because we wrestle and fight against wrong desire. Wrong desire is not sin; *acting on* wrong desire is sin.

If wrong desires were sin, then we would all be in trouble. Everyone deals with some kind of wrong desire in their lives. An essential part of walking in victory is by the grace and power of God, learning to cultivate your desires to fall in line with His Word. This may seem impossible at times, but it is absolutely possible and necessary. The psalmist gives us the essential key to unlocking this door to power living.

> Delight yourself also in the LORD, and He shall give you the desires of your heart.
> —PSALM 37:4

Does this mean God will grant us our desires even if they are in contradiction to His Word? Absolutely not. We can read this verse and think the breakthrough is at the end of it when our desires are fulfilled. But that would be wrong. The real victory of this verse is in its beginning. *When we delight ourselves in the Lord*, it has a major effect on what we desire.

"Delight" in this passage is the Hebrew word *anag*. It means to be happy about and to take exquisite delight in. When we make our life's pursuit delighting in the Lord, there is a shift in our desires. Progressively, as we delight in Him, we find true happiness and joy. God actually knows what's best for us. He knows what will bring us the most joy, peace, and fulfillment. The beautiful thing about the Lord is this: not only does He know all these things, but He also wants to give them to us!

When we start desiring what is right, we gain an incredible advantage in spiritual warfare over the enemy and over ourselves!

3. Do what is right.

It's one thing to know what is right, and it's another thing to desire what is right. But you conquer the devil when you *do* what is right. Our lives are most marked not by what we know or what we desire but by what we do. It is important to be a doer.

Being a doer does not save or redeem us. We are not saved by what we do; we are saved by what Jesus has already done. Jesus purchased our total and complete victory through His death, burial, and resurrection. We are incapable of doing anything that would save and redeem ourselves. Religion cries, "Do!" The cross declares, "Done!"

> For it is by grace you have been saved, through faith—
> and this not from yourselves, it is the gift of God.
> —EPHESIANS 2:8, NIV

We are saved by God's grace alone. But it is in the power of that grace that we rise to do what is right. Even when we are still grappling with desires that pull us toward what is wrong, God expects us to do some things.

> Be doers of the word, and not hearers only.
> —JAMES 1:22

In this text the word *doer* means, "a producer and performer." God expects us to produce and perform His Word. Something is expected of us. We hear so little of that truth today, but it is still immeasurably important. What we do matters! Victory in our lives can be thwarted if we fail to do what is right.

Religion cries, "Do!" The cross declares, "Done!"

You are no threat to the devil as long as you remain just a hearer of the Word. Satan is not upset, intimidated, or threatened by how much of God's Word you hear or know. He is not threatened when you listen to a DVD, read a book, or go to a conference. He is threatened and defeated when you become a doer of the Word!

You can do what is right even when your desires are in opposition to doing so. Jesus gave us the most profound example of this when He prayed:

> Father, if it is Your will, take this cup away from Me; nevertheless not My will, but Yours, be done.
> —LUKE 22:42

Picture the scene in your mind. Jesus is in the Garden of Gethsemane; He is facing the hardest trial and test of His life. He is about to be marred, mangled, and massacred for your sin and mine. The word *Gethsemane* means "the place of the oil press." It was the place where olives were bruised and crushed in order to retrieve their precious oil. Jesus was at the place of the oil press, under indescribable pressure. The heaviness that He was contending with cannot be described or illustrated by words on paper. He is compelled by love and the will of the Father to lay down His life in the most brutal and hellish fashion. Make no mistake: He does *not* want to do it.

In a moment of complete and utter desperation He cries out to the heavenly Father: "If You are willing, let this cup pass from Me!" He is declaring with this statement, "I really don't want to suffer. I don't want to be abused, tortured, and tormented. I don't want to hang naked on the cross before My own mother. I don't want to be humiliated. I don't want to be bruised, beaten, and bloodied. So, Father, if You could, if it's possible, let this cup pass from Me."

Jesus's next words after that statement are some of the most powerful words in the entire Bible. "*Nevertheless not My will.*" I am overwhelmed by the word *nevertheless.* I have stood on the

Mount of Olives many times in the same olive grove where Christ prayed. I stood in that sacred place and wept tears of gratitude. Two thousand years ago when Jesus said, "Nevertheless," my life was changed and a fallen world was transformed.

Jesus prayed, "Not My will." The English word translated "will" is the Greek word *thelo*. Thelo means, "to have in mind, to wish or to desire." Jesus submitted to the Father in His prayer and said, "Nevertheless, not what I have in mind, not what I desire, but what You desire." He was saying in essence, "Father, help Me break the will of man; let Me show him that he can go against the grain and overcome his flesh. Use Me to break the stubborn will of humanity. Help Me teach him that he can do what he does not want to do. He can resist the devil and require himself to submit to Your will, Father."

The thing you must know about Jesus is this: He knew His foe. He understood how to overcome the mind games of Satan. Even though Jesus didn't want to experience death on the cross, He understood that what God wanted for His life was much greater than what He desired at that moment. There is always victory and joy on the other side of doing what God has commanded.

> We do this by keeping our eyes on Jesus, the champion who initiates and perfects our faith. Because of the joy awaiting him, he endured the cross, disregarding its shame. Now he is seated in the place of honor beside God's throne.
> —HEBREWS 12:2, NLT

Joy awaits us when we do what is right! No matter what you are facing, you have an opportunity today to defeat the enemy. Even if it's hard, forgive, make the call, get things right. Fight for your family. Stand in faith. Resist the temptation. Say no to the wiles of the enemy, and say yes to the plan of God. I promise you, there is joy on the other side of submitting to the Father.

Allow the Lord to adjust your desires and infuse your mind with

His perfect plan. Overcome *you* in the equation, and you are poised to defeat your enemy the devil.

In Jesus's name you will be victorious because *you know your foe!*

Chapter 3

The FIGHT *of Your* LIFE

ANY PERSON WHO REFUSES TO ACKNOWLEDGE THE reality of spiritual warfare has been effectively enchanted by the power of hell's spells. As you read this book it is important for you to comprehend that not only are you in a fight, but also you're in the fight of your life.

> For we wrestle not against flesh and blood, but against principalities, against powers, against the rulers of the darkness of this world, against spiritual wickedness in high places.
> —Ephesians 6:12, KJV

The first three words in this scripture validate the true reality of spiritual warfare in the life of a believer: "For we wrestle." This speaks of everyone, doesn't it? Paul didn't say some people wrestle and some don't, or some wrestle and some watch. There are no spectators in spiritual warfare. The sobering fact is we all wrestle. No one—and I mean no one—is spared from engaging in spiritual warfare.

It doesn't matter how long you've been saved, how much Bible you know, what denomination you're a part of, or even how spiritual you perceive yourself to be. None of these things exempt you from this struggle. Whether you pastor a church, sell real estate, work at Chick-fil-A, or have any other vocation, you wrestle. No

1une, no one gets a free pass, and no one is left out. For 1r certain, we are *all* in this fight.

There are no spectators in spiritual warfare.
The sobering fact is we all wrestle.

It's very interesting that Paul uses the term *wrestle* here because it gives incredible insight into his philosophy of spiritual warfare. *Wrestle* is actually a very intense word as it is translated from the original Greek of the New Testament. It is the word *pale*.[1]

> **Wrestle (*pale*)**—a contest in which two opponents endeavor to gain control of one another by throwing one another. The victor is the one who gains control of his adversary's neck and pins him to the ground.

What is striking here in Paul's illustration is the fact that victory is secured over an opponent by controlling his neck. Victory didn't occur when you controlled his arm, leg, or any other part of his body, only his neck. When you control someone's neck, you control that person, because when you control someone's neck, you control how he or she perceives the world.

Think about it: with your neck you turn *to* something or *away* from something. It is through the functioning power of the neck that you determine what you look at and what you avoid looking at. Quite literally the enemy wants to control how you perceive your life and the people in it. He wants to control what you see.

You are a three-part being: you *are* a spirit, you *live* in a body, and you *have* a soul. Your soul is your mind, will, and emotions. The enemy knows if he has your soul, he has you. If he controls your mind, will, and emotions, then he controls you.

This is why we describe salvation as the saving of our souls. Surrendering our lives to Christ requires the surrender of our souls, which represents our mind, will, and emotions. The warfare you are in is for your soul—your mind, will, and emotions.

I've heard it said that the eyes are the window to the soul. If this is the case, then be careful what you show your eternal soul. A big part of spiritual warfare is not giving the devil control over what you look upon. You are wrestling and fighting for your eternity, and you cannot afford to yield access of your eye gate to the enemy. Nowadays thousands of channels are available on the television, and with the seemingly unlimited power of the Internet, disaster can be just a click away. Almost anything immoral and imaginable can be experienced instantly. Be careful. Don't get caught in a mousetrap!

Job understood the importance of not giving the devil access or control over what he looked at.

> I have made a covenant with my eyes; why then should I look upon a young woman?
>
> —Job 31:1

Those are powerful words from this ancient biblical hero. Job said, "I made a covenant, a deal, an arrangement with my eyes." He was a man who refused to surrender control of his eye gate to the enemy. Job was determined. Even though he had to contend with a nagging wife, he still refused to look at anyone else's!

There are so many troubles that arise when we yield control of our spiritual necks to the devil. When he controls what we turn toward and what we refrain from looking at, we are on the road to certain disaster. He desperately wants to control what comes into our eye gate, and this is why he wrestles and fights with us so intensely.

Metaphorically, when someone has control of your neck, he manages the way you perceive things. Perception is how you interpret and live your life. Whoever controls your neck can even restrict airflow so that you can't breathe. When you can't breathe in the natural, you become confused and disoriented. This is a very important strategy of the enemy. He will do everything he can do to keep you confused and disoriented. He fights to control your perception.

In this fight Satan wants to control your neck because he does not want you to see things clearly. He wants to dominate your perception. *Wrong perception* is a powerful weapon the enemy uses in our lives. We make our decisions based on how we perceive the world around us, and if our perception is messed up, our lives will be as well.

The enemy works very hard in the area of perception. A real simple definition for the word perception is:

> **Perception**—a way of regarding, understanding, or interpreting something

Perception is actually in the same family of words as interception or reception. It has to do with how we receive something. If we receive a right thing in a wrong way, or even a wrong thing in a right way, we are in trouble because our perception is off.

The enemy in this spiritual warfare wants to get you by the spiritual neck and cause you to perceive things incorrectly. He wants to affect your perception in matters of hope, healing, forgiveness, and breakthrough. He will do everything he can to convince you that God doesn't love you and would never move on your behalf. Satan wants you to think that your situation is hopeless and that he—not the Lord—is in control. He will attack your mind and cause you to think incorrectly. He wants you to perceive that those who are for you are against you and those who are against you are for you.

Satan wants to make you to think too much of yourself and become swollen with pride, or too little of yourself and be bound by insecurities. Satan will try to persuade you that wrong is right, right is wrong, up is down, and down is up. Every day Satan's forces work hard to affect your perception.

Years ago I saw a documentary about pilots who, while in flight, developed wrong perception. These unfortunate aviators could literally be flying straight down or severely pitched to the side yet be convinced they were flying straight ahead and level. This has happened countless times throughout the history of aviation. Most often the end result is a deadly crash landing. All this can occur when the pilot's perception is off. The period in a flight where pilots are most vulnerable is when they are navigating through dark or stormy times. This is also true as it relates to our lives. It pays to remember that Satan knows that in our darkest and stormiest seasons of life we are most vulnerable to wrong perception. When we face the dark and stormy seasons, it can have an intense effect on our ability to perceive things correctly.

Have you ever experienced times in your life when, because of the pressure you were under, you just didn't see things as clearly as you wished? In those times you can make some of your worst and most regrettable decisions. It is amazing to me how the natural and spiritual world have so many similarities. In both the natural world of flying and the spiritual realm of living there is an answer for wrong perception.

The fact is, almost all planes are equipped with instruments that inform the pilot of his level and pitch. But if the pilot is not instrument trained and certified, or if he doesn't trust his instruments, he is in trouble. In vulnerable times he stands a serious risk of crashing. Many pilots along with their passengers have died because of wrong perception. But death and tragedy could have been averted if the pilot had understood and trusted his instruments.

In our everyday life we don't have natural gauges or instruments to aid us with right perception, but we have things far greater. We have access to the Word of God and to the leading of the Holy Spirit.

Our perception is a lot like our intuition; if we are not careful, it can let us down. This is why we lean heavily on the Spirit and Word of the Lord.

As believers we have something greater than our own perception available to us; we have discernment. When God gives us discernment, we see and perceive things in a proper and right way. God gives people a true gift of discernment in ministry, and it is a powerful blessing. You may feel unqualified to have God's discernment at work in your life, but you can, because discernment is a gift. I believe that we can claim this gift as our own and have it operate in our everyday life.

Here are some of the things that occur in your life when you allow the Lord to empower you through discernment.

1. God will empower you to differentiate truth from error, right from wrong, and pure motives from impure ones.

2. You will be able to better identify deception in others.

3. You will have divine insight into determining whether a testimony attributed to God is truth or deception.

4. The Holy Spirit will enable you to recognize inaccuracies in biblical teaching and prophetic messages.

Discernment is an effective weapon in spiritual warfare, so pray for discernment. When we operate in discernment, we frustrate the schemes of the enemy in our lives. This happens because God gives us divine clarity even in dark and stormy situations. We are in no danger of crashing in hard times as long as we pay close attention to our spiritual instruments. So pray for discernment, and seek every day to know and understand the Word of the Lord.

So Who Are We Fighting?

> For we do not wrestle against flesh and blood, but against *principalities* ...
> —Ephesians 6:12, emphasis added

Now it does not take a Bible theologian to interpret the very first part of this scripture. It means exactly what it says: we are not at war with people. Anytime the church and its representatives war with people, it is totally and completely out of the will of the Lord. We miss the purpose of the cross and the message of Jesus by a mile when we war with those who are in sin, rebellion, or even opposition to us.

It is obvious that our fight is not with people. But then if we don't fight the sinner, the rebel, and the defiant to the things of God, then who or what do we fight? Paul crystallized this issue in the sixth chapter of Ephesians when he said we fight *principalities.*

> The church must never fight *with* people;
> the church must fight *for* people.

Bear in mind that Paul wrote this letter to the church in Ephesus, which was an indescribably immoral city, teeming with the most immoral people in all the Roman Empire. This city was so depraved and lawless, it was said that someone could not be legally arrested within a bowshot of the city walls. It was certainly an "anything goes community."

Ephesus was where the ancient temple dedicated to the Greek goddess Diana was located. This temple was one of the ancient wonders of the world and was an architectural marvel. Diana was considered the goddess of fertility and sexuality. Droves of temple prostitutes served the people who came into the city to worship. It was a place of darkness and wickedness, and its inhabitants were perverse and unrighteous.

Into this cesspool of a society Paul sends this letter. This amazing apostle of God was sending the church in Ephesus a reminder of where their true warfare lay. They did not war with people but rather with principalities, powers, and rulers.

Principalities

Now the Greek word for "principalities" is the word *arche*. This is a thought-provoking and interesting word that Paul used to describe those with whom we are at war. The word *principalities*, or *arche*, is defined as the first person or thing in a series. It means the beginning or first of something with more to follow.

The root word for *principalities* is the word *prince*. Jesus called the devil the prince of this world, which he is. Satan is the prince of this world of sin. Wherever sin abides, Satan reigns over it. Satan is the prince, the first of the principalities, and the principalities are demonic forces. So when Paul said we war against principalities, he was saying that we fight the devil and all that come after him—and that would be demons.

It is obvious that when you talk about a prince, you are talking about one who has power and influence. How in the world do you defeat a prince with many principalities in line just as fearsome as he? You defeat the prince and his principalities by understanding the form of government called a monarchy. A monarchy is made up of lords, princesses, princes, queens, kings, and so on.

We know that in an earthly monarchy the prince has power. But remember, no matter how much power the prince has, there is always one with more power than the prince, and that is the king. In fact, the prince only has the power that the king grants. In other words, the king has all the power.

So, who is our King? Who has all the power?

> And Jesus came and spake unto them, saying, All power
> is given unto me in heaven and in earth.
> —MATTHEW 28:18, KJV

Jesus has all power because He is the King. Most kings are born as princes. But not Jesus; when He made His entrance into this broken world, He arrived as King. Even as a baby born among barn animals and laid in a manger, He was King. All of heaven knew this and rejoiced at the King's arrival. The heavenly host certainly understood this, but they were not the only ones. Satan knew that King Jesus had been born and was afraid. He was so terrified of the Christ that he inspired Herod to attempt to kill Him.

When Jesus was born in Bethlehem, it sent shock waves through the spirit realm and shook hell all the way down to its core. Jesus was so much more than an earthly king. He was the one whom John the revelator described as "The King of kings." The psalmist David identifies our King in Psalm 24 as the King of glory.

> Lift up your heads, O you gates! And be lifted up, you everlasting doors! And the King of glory shall come in. Who is this King of glory? The LORD strong and mighty, the LORD mighty in battle. Lift up your heads, O you gates! Lift up, you everlasting doors! And the King of glory shall come in. Who is this King of glory? The LORD of hosts, He is the King of glory.
> —PSALM 24:7–10

You may be engaged in battle right now with the prince of this world and his cohorts, and if you are, it's not time to hang your head in defeat. On the contrary; *lift up your head!* The King of glory, who is mighty in battle, will come into your situation, and He has all power! When you are fighting a prince, the smartest thing to do is claim the power of the King. Use the power of the *King of kings*! King Jesus has more power than all the power of Prince Satan and all those who serve him. Jesus is strong, present, and accounted for in your battle.

Even in your hardest days attach yourself to the power of the King. You can have confidence in your King. Jesus has never had an identity crisis, and He knows exactly who He is.

> Pilate therefore said to Him [Jesus], "Are You a king then?" Jesus answered, "You say rightly that I am a king."
> —JOHN 18:37

It is not enough that Jesus be aware of who He is; that is a given. Real breakthrough power comes when you identify Him as your King who reigns over everything. He reigns over every issue, problem, and impossibility that you face. Whether it's the salvation of a loved one, a financial breakthrough, or a miracle of healing, be encouraged! Your King reigns supreme. He knows it, and you need to know it and believe.

Our warfare is made possible because we have been empowered by the King! Fight in the *King's* power! Satan can handle our power alone, but he will never be able to match the power of our King.

One of the many amazing things about our King is that He not only has all the power, but also He actually trusts us to use that divine power.

> Behold, I give you the authority to trample on serpents and scorpions, and over all the power of the enemy, and nothing shall by any means hurt you.
> —LUKE 10:19

Wow! Now that is amazing! Our King has granted us power over all the power of the enemy. In the Book of 2 Corinthians Paul describes believers in Jesus as "ambassadors for Christ" (2 Cor. 5:20). An ambassador is commissioned as a legal representative of his or her government. When the ambassador speaks, he has the weight of all his government and military forces behind him. As a believer, who is an ambassador for Christ, when you speak, you speak with power. You have all the power of heaven and all the power of your King behind you.

When we walk in submission to the will, plan, and purpose of the King in our lives, *we have power over all the power of the enemy!*

The word *authority* in Luke 10:19 is the Greek word *exousia*. *Exousia* means "the power of him whose will and commands must be submitted to or obeyed." Satan has to obey you when you operate in the power of the King. No matter how intense the level of spiritual warfare may be, don't be drawn into fear by the enemy. As a child of God you have power, and you are equipped for every fight. Whatever battle you're in right now or whatever one is to come, be encouraged; you have all you need to come out victorious.

There is, however, an important prerequisite that must be instituted before we can truly walk in the King's power. We must be submitted to the King's authority. It is important to understand that we speak and operate in and through the power of the King. As long as we remain submitted to the King, we remain empowered by the King. The moment we refuse to submit to the King we are in rebellion. Rebellion always costs dearly; it carries a price tag that demands heavenly power and authority as payment. In the kingdom of heaven power comes only one way, and that's through submission. Satan never learned that, and this is why he was stripped bare of heavenly power, authority, and influence.

Instead of walking in fear and doubt, learn to walk in faith and power. You have power over all the power of the enemy insomuch as you speak, live, and declare the mind and purpose of the King. When you do this, Satan has to submit to you.

The rulers of darkness

In Ephesians 6:12 Paul describes our struggle as a struggle with principalities, but he doesn't stop there. He adds to that powerful verse the words "against the rulers of darkness." Rulers represent Satan and demons. Darkness represents ungodliness, immorality, and sin. Satan orchestrates and holds sway over all the darkness in this world. Satan inspires every act of rebellion and sin. Gossip, rape, murder, wickedness, abuse, addiction, racism, and anything else that cause pain and dysfunction in the human race are ruled over by Satan. Satan rules in darkness, while as believers we rule in light.

As I studied the word *darkness* from the original Greek, I was captured by the intensity and severity of this word. When you apply this word to people, it is carried to another level and dimension. "Darkness" in Ephesians 6:12 is a person in whom darkness becomes visible and holds sway.

That sounds like a contradiction, doesn't it? How can darkness become visible? I started thinking about that and had to realize how incredibly accurate that description is. I have seen this manifest many times over the years in the lives of people. For example, have you ever seen someone so lost or so bound that you could see the darkness in and over their lives? It was a darkness evident even in their countenance and demeanor. And not only could you see it, but you also knew that the darkness had control and that it was in charge. You knew for sure and for certain, in that person's life, the darkness had sway.

I have personally witnessed this in the lives of believers. I have been saddened as I have seen them distance themselves from the light and presence of Jesus. In those times I have watched the darkness creep up on and in them and drive out the light. Darkness is not happy unless it is in total charge.

The truth is, not only have I *witnessed* this, but I have also *battled* this. I suppose in one way or another we all have. Yet I am grateful that we have power over the darkness; it doesn't have power over us.

We must refuse to get caught and captured by the darkness of compromise, no matter how subtle its approach or justifiable it may seem. Bitterness, compromise, sin, unforgiveness, or anything else can create darkness that can dominate our lives if we don't remain on guard and aware. God has called you to walk in the light of His Word and in the light of His presence.

> But if we walk in the light as He is in the light, we have fellowship with one another, and the blood of Jesus Christ His Son cleanses us from all sin.
> —1 JOHN 1:7

Our walk in this verse is a picture of our daily lifestyle. We walk in the light through prayer, through spending time in God's Word, and through fellowship with other believers. Spiritual warfare must be fought and won every day.

Powers

Now I saved the most intense part of this chapter for last. It's about to get real, so hang on. Paul described our warfare as warfare against *powers.*

This is actually the Greek word *exousia* as well. *Exousia* is one of those words in the Greek that has more than one meaning and application. The bulk of this scripture has been talking about the fight raging between the devil and us. But there is something very different about this part that must be brought to light. The word *power* or *exousia* can also be interpreted to mean the power of choice or the liberty of doing as one pleases.

We established earlier that the devil cannot force us to do anything. He can influence us, but he cannot force us into any act or behavior. So this power that we are promised here in this text is the most necessary power of all: God has granted me power over *me*! You have the power in this spiritual warfare over *you*! You can live a moral life and overcome compromise. You can rid your life of gossiping words, pride, unforgiveness, a critical spirit, and anger because God gives you that kind of power. God has given you power over you, because He knew you would be in the fight of your life and the greatest adversary you would face would be *you*!

Through the power of God, if I can bring Jim Raley into submission, I will overcome. The same is true for you. If you can make right choices and remain submitted to the Lord, you will win in this spiritual warfare. And Jesus has given you and me the power to do it.

We cannot afford to flirt with the darkness or mess around with compromise. God has given us the power to choose righteousness, but it is a fight. The greatest wrestling we will ever do is not with the devil but with ourselves.

God has enabled you to conquer through the power of choice. You can choose to stare down doubt, fear, sin, and compromise; get them by the neck; pin them to the ground; and tell them, "No!" You will either declare to them, "You will not have power over me in Jesus's name," or "I will submit to you." The choice belongs to the person it has always belonged to: *you*.

> The greatest wrestling we will ever do is not with the devil, but with ourselves.

Each of us is in the fight of our lives, and we must be "in it to win it" as Randy Jackson likes to say on *American Idol*. There is far too much at stake: eternity hangs in the balance, and many are depending on us. Young people are watching us, the world is waiting on us, the battle is raging, and we must choose!

Listen, my friend, you're in the fight of your life, and you must decide right now—losing is not an option!

Chapter 4

DANGEROUS DISCIPLES

GOD HAS CALLED AND EQUIPPED YOU TO BE DANGEROUS. When you fully comprehend the victory of the cross and the power of the resurrection, you become a dangerous disciple. The devil knows it, and he's banking on the fact that you won't ever discover it. Even if you feel frustrated, powerless, and spiritually weak, you are still dangerous. This is why the enemy wars against you. The only time an opponent ceases to be a threat is when he can no longer rise to fight. There is plenty of fight left in you, and all of hell knows it!

I am determined to shed light on the forgotten power that lies in a victorious church. Through the power of God you are a dangerous disciple, and you can overcome each and every one of hell's spells. Satan fights the people of God intensely because he fully comprehends the threat they actually are. He wants the church to stay dumbed down, while God desires His church to be fired up!

Even if you feel defeated right now, begin to say to yourself what your enemy, the devil, already knows. Declare it: "I am a dangerous disciple!" As a dangerous disciple it's time to discover the nature of your fight and the weapons you have at your disposal so you can dispose of your enemy!

As you read this book, I declare over your life that you are an overcomer, a victor, and more than a conqueror. This is reality for some of you and faith for others. But even if you feel as if you're losing, be encouraged; I am speaking to your destiny and potential.

Your potential is greater than your problem, your past, or anything else you may be facing right now.

We have already established that we are involved in the epic battle of the ages. We and all of heaven are engaged in spiritual warfare. The devil wants to cast a spell on you and convince you that you are not a participant, but that's a lie. Whether you like it or not, acknowledge it or not, it doesn't change the fact that it is going on.

> Your potential is greater than your problem,
> your past, or anything else
> you may be facing right now.

The devil is fighting harder and more intensely than ever, and so must we. It is time to understand something very powerful: as a disciple of Christ you are potentially a lethal weapon in the hands of the Lord against the spells and schemes of the devil.

In the Book of Ephesians Paul gives a list of the spiritual equipment made available to every believer.

> Finally, my brethren, be strong in the Lord and in the power of His might. Put on the whole armor of God, that you may be able to stand against the wiles of the devil. For we do not wrestle against flesh and blood, but against principalities, against powers, against the rulers of the darkness of this age, against spiritual hosts of wickedness in the heavenly places. Therefore take up the whole armor of God, that you may be able to withstand in the evil day, and having done all, to stand. Stand therefore, having girded your waist with truth, having put on the breastplate of righteousness, and having shod your feet with the preparation of the gospel of peace; above all, taking the shield of faith with which you will

be able to quench all the fiery darts of the wicked one. And take the helmet of salvation, and the sword of the Spirit, which is the word of God; praying always with all prayer and supplication in the Spirit, being watchful to this end with all perseverance and supplication for all the saints.

—EPHESIANS 6:10–18

Do you want to be a dangerous disciple of the Lord? Part of becoming one is to understand your spiritual weapons. Paul wanted his children in the faith to be equipped to handle every attack of the devil. He understood where they were vulnerable (as we are) and wanted them to be protected. Since we have already established that this is spiritual warfare, then it is only logical to assume this fact: *to fight a spiritual battle requires the use of spiritual weapons.*

LET'S GET READY TO RUMBLE

Paul writes to the church in Ephesus describing the whole armor of God. He uses natural weaponry and armor to illustrate powerful spiritual truths in this letter. He was a brilliant teacher because he applied natural, relatable, everyday, understandable things to make spiritual points.

Finally, my brethren, be strong in the Lord and in the power of His might.

—EPHESIANS 6:10

Paul's instructions to the church in Ephesus two thousand years ago are still appropriate for us today. *Be strong in the Lord.* In order to overcome hell's spells and win in this spiritual battle, it will require strength from the Lord.

Remember, Paul established in the twelfth verse that this is not a battle with flesh and blood, and since this is not a natural fight, we won't win it with natural weapons. It would be like bringing a knife to a gunfight. We find ourselves in deep trouble when we try to fight a spiritual fight with natural weapons.

This is why Paul said, "Be strong in the Lord." In other words, for this fight, what has worked for you in the past will not work for you now. Your money, skills, possessions, abilities, training, knowledge, confidence, or anything else you possess will not be sufficient for these types of battles.

I have been there many times. It's a place where we realize that in and of ourselves we are totally insufficient. Whether it is an intense family situation, health crisis, financial issue, or something else, those times find us all. In those moments of impossibility we discover we need the power of God.

Paul told his friends and spiritual children something very powerful in the onset of verse 10. He simply said, "Be strong." Make no mistake about it: to overcome the spirit of the age you will be required to be strong. A closer look at the word *strong* as it is used here in verse 10 reveals a couple of amazing things.

Strong in this context means to receive strength, to be endued and equipped with strength. The point is, this is strength we don't inherently possess. This is a kind of strength we are not born with. This strength comes from another world. You might be wondering how to receive this kind of otherworldly strength. You can't earn it, buy it, or be good enough to deserve it. You gain this strength one way and one way only: through the grace of God.

If we had to earn God's strength or measure up to deserve it, we would all fall incredibly short. God gives us strength in tough times because He loves us.

It's very powerful and interesting to me that Paul's instructions include not just being strong, but being strong *in the Lord*.

When someone is a lord, it means they are an owner, possessor, and the one who has control. I am grateful that the one who is our Lord and has the strength is the one who is willing to give it, grant it, and bestow it on His people. So since it's His strength and He is the owner and possessor of this power, if He is giving His strength, then we should be receiving it!

God has provided you with everything you need to annihilate, devastate, and obliterate Satan and his forces. Now I want you to picture in your mind's eye a strong and powerful soldier standing before you from the time of Paul. A Roman soldier in those days was arrayed with both offensive and defensive weapons. Paul systematically identifies each piece of a soldier's natural gear and paints an incredible picture of the incredible spiritual power you and I have available to us.

We must apply and utilize everything God has made available to us. In doing so we become impregnable to the attack of the devil and walk above the power of hell's spells!

1. Put on the belt of truth.

Let's take a close look at the soldier's belt. In the natural sense his belt was a very important part of his battle array. It was a large piece of leather with thick cut strands of leather that had bits of metal attached to the strands. The belt covered his stomach and abdomen as well as his groin and reproductive regions. A soldier's belt acted as a type of shield and protection for vital areas.

The first part for the soldier affected and protected by his belt was his stomach. Whenever the Bible talks about your stomach or your belly in a spiritual sense, it is talking about your inner self or your inner being. It's who you are and what you believe and feel deep down inside. One of the ways the enemy most desires to affect you is by sowing seeds of doubt and lies deep down inside of you.

Whatever gets deep down inside of a person, truth or lie, becomes extremely hard to dislodge. The enemy knows something very important: we all live our lives based on what we believe. He knows if he can hoodwink you, he can swindle away the life of victory God has for you and replace it with a life of defeat. Truth is essential in overcoming hell's spells of deception.

In a world filled with lies and deception, it pays to get truth deep down in your belly—so deep that you will not be misled by the lies of the devil.

> Behold, You desire truth in the inward parts.
> —PSALM 51:6

The very goal and plan of God is that you would be filled with truth deep down inside. When you have truth deep down inside of yourself, you are not so easily moved by the lies and the attacks of Satan. Deep-down truth will cause you to become impervious to the lies of the devil!

The enemy knows something very important: we all live our lives based on what we believe.

When you talk about something being in your belly, it's deep down inside of you. There is great protection in truth, and you must protect the truth that has been placed inside of you. The only way we will truly have a stomach for spiritual warfare and the power to break hell's spells is to get truth deep down inside of us!

The belt the soldier wore also protected his reproductive area. It protected his ability to be able to participate in birthing what had been placed inside of him. To me that represents that our potential is protected by truth.

The enemy wants to assault the truth in your life with a lie because he knows, if and when he can, he will destroy your ability to be productive. Unless we make truth our foundation, our next season in God will never be birthed! When Satan robs of us the truth of the Lord in our lives, we become sterile and unable to birth what God has placed within us.

Have you ever seen individuals bound by so many lies that they could never really accomplish anything much in their lives? They were bound by the lie that they could never get past their past, never accomplish anything significant in their present, and never see their dreams fulfilled in their future. How many people are barren and impotent, unable to birth anything for God's glory because they have allowed the enemy to deceive them?

Deception leads to disaster, every time.

If you are grappling with these issues even now, shake loose from the lies of the devil and hear this truth: *You can do and become everything that God has placed within you!* God is on your side, He is for you and not against you, and it's time to receive truth in your belly and get ready to birth the next season!

Truth is critical for where you are called to go and what you are called to do. This is why you must remain committed to hearing and receiving truth.

Something else very significant here is the fact that a belt holds everything up. We see that fact illustrated by so many young men who walk around today with their pants falling off! Without a belt everything fails and falls.

It is truth that holds everything up. In fact, almost every other part of the soldier's weaponry in one way or another was attached to the belt.

Everything in your life is attached to the truth you know, hear, and receive.

The level of victory and breakthrough you live in is all linked to the truth that you comprehend. Your spiritual, emotional, and even financial well-being is attached to the truth you embrace. This is why to live without truth in your life is not an option. Everything is held in place by truth.

Most importantly your eternity is based on the truth you embrace. We need to hear and receive truth. In Isaiah 59:4 the prophet Isaiah said that there would come a time when no one would plead for truth.

Much of the church is spellbound, fascinated, and charmed to such a degree that they don't even desire truth. Truth has become relative rather than absolute. This would mean (in the minds of many) that the Bible is truth, but it is only relative truth, not absolute truth. That means truth changes according to our situation. Situational ethics and relative truth would say nothing is completely right all the time and nothing is completely wrong all the time; it all changes according to whatever the situation may be. This is so wrong and incredibly dangerous.

> No one calls for justice, nor does any plead for truth.
> They trust in empty words and speak lies; they conceive evil and bring forth iniquity.
> —ISAIAH 59:4

Plead for truth! We need truth in our nation, truth in our homes, and truth in our lives. There is protection in truth! We need truth spoken in the pulpits and churches in America today as never before.

I am blessed to pastor an incredible church. We strive to be creative and cutting edge. We make intense efforts to be relevant, but we refuse to compromise on truth. To be relevant without truth is to be irrelevant. The church that is relevant without being revolutionary is wasting its time. The truth that we possess makes us both relevant and revolutionary.

A soldier's belt held the sheath for the sword, and without the belt of truth the sword of the Word will not have power in our lives. Truth will stand when everything else is falling around us. Gird yourself with truth!

2. Put on the breastplate of righteousness.

The breastplate was an important article of defense that protected the front torso and vital organs from a mortal wound. It was often composed of a solid piece of metal, but it could also contain numerous small pieces of metal that were sewn to cloth or leather that overlapped much like the scales of a fish. These scales could number as many as seven hundred to one thousand per breastplate.

When the sun shone directly on the armor, it would become

very hot. To avoid being burned (or even pinched) by the moving metal plates, the soldiers always wore a sturdy robe under the armor. Don't miss this truth: *the breastplate functioned because of what was going on underneath it.*

Even though the breastplate was visible, there was a robe under it. What was on the outside of the soldier could not have functioned without what was going on underneath.

We reveal the breastplate of righteousness when we have on the robe of righteousness, the righteousness of the Lord Jesus covering our lives. Righteousness starts on the inside and then manifests on the outside. Before we ever live righteously without, we must be transformed by Christ's righteousness within. Righteous living is just an outward manifestation of an inward condition. It is that inner robe of righteousness that will keep us faithful in our marriages, honest in our dealings, and guarding our actions.

The breastplate protected the soldier's heart—and make no mistake about it, the enemy wants to deliver a mortal wound to your heart. Metaphorically the heart always represents the place of emotions, feeling, and discernment. The enemy is after your heart.

The longer I serve the Lord, the more I realize how important it is to protect my heart. It is very easy to allow things to penetrate our hearts, and once they are there, they are hard to remove. The enemy will shoot arrows of bitterness, judgmentalism, criticalness, unforgiveness, and poison at our hearts. This is why we must guard our hearts.

When the devil can get you to a place where you will receive negative and harmful things into your heart, he has cast a spell on you. Don't allow yourself to be drawn into his trap, but keep your heart.

> Keep your heart with all diligence, for out of it spring the issues of life.
> —PROVERBS 4:23

It's imperative to understand that your heart is under constant attack. The enemy wants to get to your heart, because he knows that when he gets to your heart, he gets to you! If he is allowed to influence and penetrate your heart, he has gained access to your behavior, your hopes, and even your dreams.

If the enemy gets hold of your heart, it becomes a breeding ground for bitterness and unforgiveness. You become a person who is easily offended. Once you pick up an offense from someone, you cut that person off and hold that thing against them. Maybe it was one big thing, or maybe it's many small things that you keep a list of in your heart. That other person may not even be aware they've done something, but you choose to be offended and unforgiving instead of working things out. I heard it said one time, "Don't cut a rope when you can untangle a knot." Forgiveness goes a long way in untangling knotted-up relationships. But if you don't guard your heart, unforgiveness will take root at the cost of your relationships.

Solomon said to guard your heart because it is the wellspring of life. It's the source of everything you do. If you lose heart, you have lost it all. You lose your focus, your energy, and your passion for the things of God. So I echo Solomon in urging you to guard your heart. Don't lose heart in your relationship with the Lord. Don't lose heart and give up on your family; don't lose heart on your potential and calling. Guard your heart, my friend.

Even as it relates to your health, nothing matters more than your heart. I don't care how healthy every other part of your body is; if your heart is sick, weak, and vulnerable, you cannot survive. It's the same in the spiritual realm: your heart is critical to your spiritual survival. Wearing the breastplate of righteousness is an effectual spiritual defense for your heart.

You might be wondering what righteousness looks like. Righteousness means having right motives, right actions, and right behavior—all of these things follow the person who is committed to equipping himself with the breastplate of righteousness. But more importantly Jesus gives us His righteousness, which far surpasses our own. Through the love and mercy of Jesus we can have right standing with God, and our hearts are protected.

3. Put on shoes of peace.

Proper footwear was a powerful and practical part of a Roman soldier's attire. Did you know that the best and most highly trained foot soldier is only as good as the shoes he's wearing? If a soldier injures his feet, he stops making progress and can no longer fight. So it's certainly not an accident that Paul instructed the New Testament believers to wear shoes of peace.

In spiritual warfare the enemy will attack our peace because he knows if he can rob us of peace, we will cease to make progress and will be unfit to fight. Many times the enemy has affected us in such a way that rather than walking in peace, we are tormented by trouble and paralyzed by our own pain. Have you ever been paralyzed by your own pain? A lack of peace will leave us frozen and unable to embark upon God's assignments for us. The truth is, when your feet hurt, everything hurts! You can't walk; you can't enjoy the moment; you can't think about anything else but the pain. You just want to sit down.

Roman soldiers were amazing fighters, and they were famous for their long marches. In fact, they were so prolific at marching that it was often a great shock to their enemies. Roman soldiers would keep marching when their foes were convinced they were hunkered down and resting. I read that there have been occasions when Caesar's army marched one hundred miles at a time. You're probably thinking, "How in the world?" Certainly the Roman soldier was strong, well trained, and determined. That definitely had a great deal to do with his success, but there is more to it than just that. A Roman soldier's ability to march for such great distances was directly related to the amazing shoes he wore.

There are some interesting facts about a Roman soldier's shoes, and it would be wise to note them: a soldier's shoes were light, flexible, and resilient. If you want to conquer in spiritual warfare, you must learn to live a life similar to the soldier's shoes. You experience the most peace when you learn to live your life in a light, flexible, and resilient fashion.

Live lightly. What I mean by being light is this: live your life without heaviness. Don't get weighted down by the cares of this world in constantly trying to please or impress others. The Bible tells us in Isaiah 61:3 that God has provided us a garment of praise rather than a spirit of heaviness. Praising God will bring peace into your situation.

In contrast, focusing on yourself brings heaviness. Don't be tempted by pride or jealousy and spend yourself into debt because you care too much about what others think. Live a life that is light and uncontrolled by peer pressure.

A Roman soldier didn't wear wooden clogs; he wore shoes that were light! Don't get bogged down or clogged down, but live a light life, free from the weight of this world that would hinder you from walking in the peace of the Lord.

Live flexibly. A Roman soldier's shoes were flexible; this is a critical component to walking in the peace of the Lord. When your shoes are rigid and inflexible in the natural, it makes it very difficult to make any progress. A few years ago I was at a meeting in Denver, and we were staying at a hotel less than a mile from the convention center. It was an easy and pleasant walk. I was convinced of this until I wore the wrong shoes! I had gotten a new pair of shoes that were quite stylish but hard, rigid, inflexible, and didn't fit well. By the time I arrived at the convention center, I had rubbed great big blisters on my feet and was limping around trying to get to the meetings in that massive complex. It was embarrassing, because the only way I could make any progress at all was to take my shoes completely off! Finally I just gave up and called my wife and asked her to please bring me some better shoes. Flexible shoes matter when you want to make progress.

If you can learn to be flexible, you will walk through life with a lot more peace! I have a saying: "Blessed are the flexible, for they shall not drive the rest of us crazy!" In your own home if you are rigid, unbending, and totally unyielding, it creates an atmosphere devoid of true peace. When we are flexible, we spend a lot less time aggravated and uptight, and we are much easier to love.

One of the greatest hindrances to the plan of God in the world today is inflexible, moody, aggravated Christians. Church folk who are not flexible and who are determined to have everything their way no matter the cost are often tools the enemy uses to hold entire ministries hostage. Inflexible, rigid churches have an uncomfortable atmosphere and make very little progress.

The church I am blessed to pastor is radically committed to outreach and is one of the most flexible churches in the nation, but it hasn't always been that way. Our bus ministry brings in droves of homeless and hungry folk every single Sunday. We call them the VIPs of our church. But long before our church touched the thousands of people it touches now, we were much, much smaller. In those days we began ministry to the homeless. Early on we had some church members who were rigid, inflexible, and resistant. They struggled greatly with the direction the Lord was taking our ministry in that regard. To bring in hundreds of hurting, fractured, people—many who were struggling with addictions and other serious issues—was intense. It made for an atmosphere of stress and disunity.

I was so burdened about this. One Sunday I preached a message on servanthood. The message was entitled, "A Title or a Towel." The question I asked our congregation that day was, "What are you seeking, a title or a towel?" The towel represents the humility and servanthood that was modeled for us by Jesus washing the feet of His disciples. Jesus, the King of the ages and the Lord of all, washed the feet of those who would abandon, betray, and walk away from Him in His darkest hour. Yet He served them and washed their feet. Jesus did the job of the lowliest servant of His day. The humble act of washing feet was considered such a dirty and debasing job that a

Jewish citizen could not even be required to do it. But Jesus did. He humbled himself. Talk about flexibility!

I taught several points, and at the end of the message, I slipped off my coat, tucked a towel in my belt, and went into the audience and brought out a homeless man. I grabbed a pale full of water, slipped off his tattered shoes and his dirty socks, and began washing his feet. As I did, I began to repent for my church. I asked him to forgive us if we ever made him feel like he wasn't welcome in our gatherings. I asked him to please forgive us if we ever acted as if God loved us one little bit more than He loved him. I was weeping, he was weeping, and brokenness swept our entire congregation. People fell to their knees, some even lay on their faces, and you could hear their tearful cries of repentance echoing through our sanctuary. Something very powerful happened that day; our church became flexible, unified, and peaceful.

Examine your heart right now. If you have a tendency to be rigid and inflexible, why not ask the Lord to forgive you? Remind yourself of the many times others have been flexible with you and the many times Jesus has as well. Break the power of the enemy off of your life and walk out your faith in shoes of peace.

Live resiliently. The word *resilient* means to bounce back into shape after being bent, stretched, or compressed. One of the main keys to living your life in the peace of God is learning to be resilient. A soldier's shoes maintained their integrity even when the pressure was on. There is a lot of peace that can be derived from being resilient!

The person who is resilient is the person who bounces back from adversity and tough times. Such individuals forgive easily and refuse to allow bitterness and anger to bend them out of shape. Instead of being defined by the pressures and struggles you have endured and getting bent out of shape, be resilient and bounce back! God still has a plan for you, and He has everything under control. Claim God's peace and walk in it, in Jesus's name.

Stand your ground. Before I move on to our next piece of spiritual armor, I want to share one more very interesting fact I discovered about the shoes of Roman soldiers: they had *nails* attached to the soles of their shoes. The metal spikes resembled cleats like the ones a baseball player would wear today. In times of great warfare their shoes enabled them to stand their ground. They would dig in with their shoes and engage in the fight.

There are times when your shoes of peace will actually be a great aid to you in warfare by helping you to stand your ground. It may not always be easy, but when you know you have heard God, there is great peace that accompanies the act of standing your ground.

The enemy is all about attacking you in such a way that you are constantly losing ground. Have you ever gone through seemingly unending seasons of attack and it seemed as if you could not hold your ground? Satan understands this fact for sure; you cannot fight if you cannot stand your ground. As you read this book, even now claim the very peace of Jesus over every situation and stand your ground!

Dig in, plant your feet, and stand your ground. Stand your ground for your family, your health, your financial breakthrough, your marriage, or anything else you're fighting for. In spiritual warfare, just as in natural warfare, we must stand our ground. Even when the battle was raging, the Roman soldier was able to stand his ground because he had on the right shoes. I declare over you the kind of anointing that will enable you to wear shoes of peace and stand your ground!

You ask, "What does spiritual warfare have to do with peace?" It seems like a dichotomy, but every soldier who fights in the natural knows he is at war for peace. Sometimes you have to war for your peace. I want to encourage you in the Lord, stand your ground. Don't allow the enemy to steal that peace.

The world is desperate to see a church that will stand its ground. We must remain true and faithful in our love for God and commitment to His Word. If we hope to create lasting change, we must stand our ground!

I declare the peace of God over your life as you stand your ground in Jesus's name. Make peace with your past, possess peace in your present, and pursue peace in your future. Jesus said that was a great key to your blessing.

> Blessed (enjoying enviable happiness, spiritually prosperous—with life-joy and satisfaction in God's favor and salvation, regardless of their outward conditions) are the makers and maintainers of peace, for they shall be called the sons of God!
> —MATTHEW 5:9, AMP

I just love that, don't you?

4. Put on the helmet of salvation.

The helmet protected the Roman soldier's head. In ancient warfare a soldier's head was the most vulnerable part of his body. The same is true today; even with all the modern technology that is available on the battlefield, the head of a soldier is still in the most danger. In present-day infantry engagements, most fatal wounds are head wounds. A soldier is more likely to perish from a head wound than through any other kind of injury. In the heat of the battle protection of a soldier's head is a matter of life and death.

Our lives will change when our minds are changed.

Realizing this, it's not hard to understand why Paul emphasized that as believers we should wear the helmet of salvation. The head holds the mind, so the same way a helmet protects a soldier's head, our spiritual helmet of salvation guards our minds. We think with our minds—and what we think is very important!

When Paul described the helmet as a helmet of salvation, he

painted a very pertinent picture. It is important to have a saved mind. The mind is the ultimate theater of battle engagement. There is no battlefield that compares to the battlefield of the mind. We think, reason, and make our decisions through our thought processes. If we don't have a salvation mind-set, we are in serious trouble. Thinking right is imperative to a victorious life. The wisest man who ever lived understood this. Solomon penned these timeless words three thousand years ago, and they are just as applicable today as ever:

> As he [a man] thinks...so is he.
> —PROVERBS 23:7

Whatever you think about, you are progressively becoming. Everything anyone ever became—good or bad, positive or negative—they thought their way into. When your mind is filled with negativity, rebellion, and sin, sooner or later your life will manifest what is in your mind. Because "as [a man] thinks...so is he." But on the flip side of that, when you think positive, victorious, faith-filled thoughts that translate into similar actions, your life becomes one of victory, power, and virtue.

This is why it is so important to have a salvation mind-set. Your mind is where the victory is won or lost in your life. Listen to what Jesus said about your mind.

> "You shall love the LORD your God with all your heart, with all your soul, and with all your mind." This is the first and great commandment.
> —MATTHEW 22:37–38

Jesus insists that you love God with your *entire* mind. Just a portion or part won't do; He desires for you to love the Lord totally—so much so that in every decision, situation, and circumstance your love for Him guards and governs your mind. Could you imagine how much peace and favor you would walk in if your love for the

Lord saturated your mind and permeated your life? What if you made your love for Him the guiding force for every decision and action? Your life would be filled with so much more peace, forgiveness, love, and victory. One of the major keys to overcoming the schemes and spells of hell is a saved mind that's in love with Jesus.

Mark and Luke both record the miracle of Christ delivering a demon-possessed man (Mark 5:1–20; Luke 8:26–39). He was living his tormented life, running naked in a graveyard and mutilating himself. But one day he met Jesus, and everything changed. By the time Jesus had finished with him, the Bible says he was clothed and in his right mind. Everything changed, especially his mind. Jesus can still touch our minds.

Whatever you think about, you are progressively becoming.

It doesn't matter how messed up a mind is or how long it's been filled with sin, darkness, and confusion. Jesus is in the mind-changing business. The Bible says that the demon-possessed man was in his right mind. The phrase "right mind" is translated into English from the Greek word *sophroneo*. This word means to have a sound mind, to exercise self-control, and to curb one's passions. What cannot be denied is this: when Jesus changed the man's mind, He changed the man's life. Our lives will change when our minds are changed.

Paul told the Christians in Rome that they must not be conformed to the mind-set of the world around them, but they must be *transformed* by the *renewal* of their minds. (See Romans 12:2.) Either your thinking is made new by God's mighty touch, or you are stuck in a mentality that blindly keeps on rationalizing the delusions and depravities of a world that contradicts the truth of God every day.

Peter urges us to "gird up" our minds (1 Pet. 1:13). The usual expression found in the Bible is "gird up one's loins." In biblical times people wore calf-length robes. If they had to do something vigorous, they picked up the back of their robe, brought it forward between their legs, and tucked it into their belt. People girded their loins when they were about to do one of three things: work, run, or fight. When Peter told us to gird up our *minds*, he meant that we must think intensely and with precision. Our thinking has to tell us whether we are to work, flee, or fight a spiritual fight.

It takes wisdom to survive—even triumph—in the midst of spiritual warfare. Wisdom from heaven is what you should pursue. The enemy is determined to fill your mind with wrong and negative thoughts! So you have the responsibility as you engage in spiritual warfare to gird up your mind.

God has called you to guard your mind because you must be cognizant of this fact and reality: nobody plays mind games as well as the devil! The helmet of salvation is your great protection. The right mind, renewed by Christ, is the mind of salvation and victory.

In this crazy world the devil is launching assault after assault against the minds of believers. This is why today more than ever you must apply the helmet of salvation. How many people have died because of what I call "spiritual blunt force trauma," which is a spiritual blow to an unprotected mind? If you don't guard your mind with salvation's helmet, *all is lost!*

> But I see another law in my members, warring against
> the law of my mind...
> —ROMANS 7:23

Never forget: there is a war for your mind going on at all times! Even Paul warred with and in his own mind! He said, "I have incredible resistance from my own body that fights with my mind even when I know to do what's right!" Paul understood that it was a strong faith-filled, salvation mind-set that would keep his fleshly desires and actions under control.

You and I must wear the helmet of salvation! Wear the helmet of salvation, and when the enemy attacks your mind, declare in faith, "I am too saved to be swayed!"

5. Put on the shield of faith.

We need the shield of faith if we hope to become dangerous disciples and walk victoriously over all of hell's spells. The need for a shield shows us something very important that must be learned concerning spiritual warfare. Life is a battleground, not a playground. Hell is playing for keeps. It takes faith to survive, and it requires faith to win.

> Above all, taking the shield of faith with which you will be able to quench all the fiery darts of the wicked one.
> —EPHESIANS 6:16

There are many lessons we can learn about spiritual warfare by taking an up-close and personal look at the shield of faith. A Roman soldier's shield was a critical and necessary part of his battlefield gear. The shield he carried was quite large, usually four feet by two feet. It was handcrafted, made of wood, and covered with tough leather. The soldier kept it in front of him, and it protected him from swords, spears, and fiery darts.

Paul calls the shield for spiritual warfare the shield of faith. This is our defensive weapon, which protects us from Satan's fiery darts and attacks. Quite honestly, there are some assaults in life that will not be survived without faith. The enemy is heartless and cruel. The devil shoots fiery darts at our hearts and minds, manifesting in any and all kinds of outrageous attacks. He will attack our health, families, finances, peace of mind, and anything else. It is through and by faith that we overcome him.

> The just shall live by faith.
> —ROMANS 1:17

If we are going to live victoriously, we must live *by faith*! Faith must become our lifestyle. When we live by faith, the attacks of the enemy don't have such devastating effects on us, because faith is our protection.

The shield of faith is described as being able to quench all the fiery darts of the devil. This concept is made more powerful with a proper understanding of ancient warfare. One day some enemies of Rome dipped arrows in pitch, set the pitch on fire, and then shot the flaming arrows at Roman soldiers who were still over one hundred yards away. The arrows stuck right in the wood and leather shields the soldiers carried and set them on fire. As soon as the soldiers dropped their burning shields, the next volley of arrows killed them.

At first this strategy of warfare seemed devastating to the Roman army. How could they resist this type of attack? They had to endure arrows—and not only arrows, but *fiery* arrows. Have you ever endured seasons of attack from the devil that were not just normal attacks, but they were fiery attacks?

In their desperation the soldiers came up with an ingenious yet simple solution. They began soaking their shields in water before the battle. As soon as the fiery darts hit the water-soaked shields, the arrows hissed out. The Roman line survived and conquered their enemies.

The apostle Paul says in Ephesians 5:26 that we are sanctified and cleansed through the washing of the water by the Word. In other words, when our faith becomes saturated with the water of God's Word, it doesn't matter what fiery darts Satan sends our way; we extinguish them. Our Word-filled and faith-filled life will put out the fiery darts and attacks of the enemy! I challenge you, especially if you have been enduring a season of attack, to soak your life in God's presence and Word. When you do this, the very next thing you need to do is simply this: watch God work!

A Roman soldier carried his shield on his left arm. It protected two-thirds of his body, but that was not all. His shield also protected one-third of the body of the fellow soldier on his left. This is very significant, because every soldier was responsible for offering a measure of protection for his comrade. "Be sure you take faith as your shield," was Paul's instruction, and it is urgently important that we comply. We *must* take faith as our shield, not only because faith extinguishes the flaming missiles by which we are assaulted but also because each person's faith affords a measure of protection to others in his or her life.

The devil does not fear a big church; he fears a united one!

If I don't take up the shield of faith, it could result in disaster. You could be dangerously vulnerable to the enemy's assault on account of my carelessness and disregard. In the body of Christ we owe each other as much protection as we can give each other. After all, we are not isolated in our issues or strangers in our struggles. We are one body, one family, one community, and one fellowship.

These ancient shields were constructed in such a way that an entire line could interlock together. This enabled the soldiers to march into battle like a solid wall! Do you realize how much power we have against the enemy when we come together in faith? We are at our most lethal when we become and remain united. Satan's greatest fear is realized when believers come together in faith. The Word of God says that one can put a thousand to flight, but two can chase ten thousand (Deut. 32:30). The devil does not fear a big church; he fears a united one!

There needs to be a literal wall of faith around the people of God. You are to take up your shield of faith, but realize that you don't take it up alone. We must take it up together, and in Jesus's mighty name, no weapon formed against us shall be able to prosper.

6. *Take up the sword of the Spirit.*

The sword was the most common weapon in battle. The word *sword* appears 449 times in Scripture. All the armaments in God's spiritual arsenal are defensive in nature, but the sword is primarily an offensive weapon. In fact, the sword of God's Word is what Jesus used to overcome the devil in the wilderness, and it also gave the beast of Revelation 13 a deadly wound. When we speak of the sword in a spiritual context, we are talking about the Word of the Lord.

> For the word of God is living and powerful, and sharper than any two-edged sword, piercing even to the division of soul and spirit, and of joints and marrow, and is a discerner of the thoughts and intents of the heart.
> —HEBREWS 4:12

I believe the two edges of the Spirit's sword represent the New and Old Testaments of God's Word. You are a most dangerous disciple when you are armed with your spiritual sword and know how to use it. God's Word is also described as a two-edged sword because it is to be used both against the enemy and for personal use. It was the same with the sword of a Roman soldier. He used his sword to fight his enemy, but he also used it in his personal everyday life. His sword was critical to his survival.

Ancient soldiers also used their swords in preparing their meals. A sword was used to cut meat and vegetables and to aid in cooking. One of the best ways to get your spiritual life "cooking" is to use your sword—get filled with the Word of God, live it, declare it, wield it, and see how mightily things begin to come together in this recipe of events we call life.

The soldier also used his sword to start a fire. He needed it to split kindling wood in preparation for his fire. Most believers would tell you that they want to live lives that are on fire for the Lord. But the fire of God does not come to us until and unless the Word of God has prepared the way. I am always very cautious in embracing any supposed outpouring of God's Spirit and fire that does not have as its foundation the Word of the Lord. The sword always prepares for the fire and presence of God. The fire will only touch what the sword has made ready.

The real key to living a consistently fired-up life for God is to live a life that is daily affected by the sword of His Word.

The sword was used for setting captives free by cutting the ropes that bound them. Never forget, the sword of the Word can still set the captives free! Nothing will free captives bound by sin and shackles as will the Word of the Lord.

Time and again through the years I have seen people gloriously liberated through the power of God's Word. I have seen individuals in so much bondage that it seemed absolutely impossible they would ever be free. They have been held captive by more issues than I could ever list—drugs, sexual sin, unforgiveness, religion, and so much more. But as they came into contact with and encountered God's Word, they were supernaturally set free.

It doesn't matter what you or someone you love is in bondage to; there is deliverance free and clear through the power of God's Word. There is no substitute for the Word of the Lord. Christian music is awesome, Christian classes are an incredible blessing, and the ministry of Christian leaders is a tremendous asset. But there is nothing more impactful than the Word.

The Word is a declaration of what God has said to His people, and there is nothing more powerful than that. When it is preached and proclaimed, those who are entangled, wrangled, and strangled by sin are supernaturally set free! The Word of God is a practical tool for every area of life as well as in fighting the devil.

SHARPENING YOUR EDGE

In Bible times there was no stainless steel. Because of this a sword that was uncared for became rusty, dull, and pitted. Swords were kept clean and sharp in a number of different ways; honing them against a stone or another soldier's sword and other sharpening techniques were used to keep swords sharp and battle ready. In the same way natural soldiers needed to sharpen their natural swords, we as believers must sharpen our spiritual swords.

> Iron sharpens iron…
> —PROVERBS 27:17

It is imperative to understand that when we study the Bible with others, our skill in the Word is sharpened. In fact, you are sharpening your sword right now, and it is one of the smartest things you can do! You are preparing and learning how to better use your sword in battle against the enemy and to break the power of hell's spells!

Remember, a Roman soldier's sword was two-edged and sharp, and so is the Word of the Lord. Look again at what the writer to the Hebrews said.

> For the word of God is living and powerful, and sharper than any two-edged sword, piercing even to the division of soul and spirit, and of joints and marrow, and is a discerner of the thoughts and intents of the heart.
> —HEBREWS 4:12

A material sword pierces the body, but the Word of God pierces the heart! The more you use a physical sword, the duller it becomes. But the more you use your spiritual sword, God's Word, the sharper it becomes. You need to pull it out and read it every day.

When you encounter battles with the devil, take out your sword. Declare what God's Word says about your situation. God's Word will defeat the devil.

- Use your sword against sickness and declare, "With the stripes of Jesus I am healed!" (Isa. 53:5).

- Use your sword to confront every attack from hell and confess, "No weapon formed against me shall prosper!" (Isa. 54:17).

- When depression tries to take hold of you, grab your sword and testify, "The joy of the Lord is my strength" (Neh. 8:10).

- When the enemy tries to convince you that your family will perish without knowing or serving God, grab your sword and speak the Word: "As for me and my house, *we will serve the Lord!*" (Josh. 24:15, emphasis added).

Whatever the occasion and whatever the nature of the fight, take your sword and use it in the name of the Lord. You're in God's spiritual army now, and there is no denying it. Don't be fearful and apprehensive. You have been informed afresh and stirred toward the battle. There is only one thing left to do as a dangerous disciple!

> Therefore take up the whole armor of God, that you may be able to withstand in the evil day, and having done all, to stand.
> —EPHESIANS 6:13

Don't you dare allow the enemy to talk you out of who and what you are. When you put on the whole armor of God and wield the sword of God's powerful Word, you are a dangerous disciple! Refuse every pitiful attempt of the enemy to lessen your position of power and authority. When he tries—and he will—pull out your sword and declare, "Greater is He that is in me than he that is in the world! I am a *dangerous disciple*, fully protected, fully armed, and fully ready!" So let's fight!

Section II
BREAKING HELL'S SPELLS

Chapter Five

The CHARMED CHURCH

L ISTEN TO THIS INDICTMENT PAUL LEVELS AGAINST THE
church of Galatia.

> O foolish Galatians! *Who has bewitched you* that you
> should not obey the truth, before whose eyes Jesus
> Christ was clearly portrayed among you as crucified?
> —GALATIANS 3:1, EMPHASIS ADDED

> Oh, foolish Galatians! What magician has hypnotized
> you and cast an evil spell upon you? For you used to see
> the meaning of Jesus Christ's death as clearly as though
> I had waved a placard before you with a picture on it of
> Christ dying on the cross.
> —GALATIANS 3:1, TLB

He accuses them of being "bewitched." As I stated in the
Introduction, I wanted to use two different translations in order to
reveal the fact to you that hell's spells are real and can be present in
the church. And to reiterate, the word *bewitched* used in the New
King James Version means the act of casting a spell, to charm, to
fascinate, and to please to such a degree as to take away the power
of resistance.

How in the world can the power and influence of hell's spells
exist in the church? It seems preposterous that anything like this
could ever manifest among the people of God. To gain a clear

understanding of how this occurs, we need to do a behind-the-scenes look at the churches in Galatia and discover exactly why Paul would make such an outrageous claim and write such a letter.

First of all, Paul greatly loved these people. He had been their founding pastor and was a spiritual father to them. He had brought them the power of the gospel of Jesus Christ. He shared his life-changing message with them unfiltered by religion and unhindered by any hidden agenda.

Paul pioneered this church on his second missionary journey into Asia Minor. He started with a group of people who had their religious roots in idolatry. The church was made up of Gentile converts who had come from a background of pagan practices. Just take a glance at what they were before Paul led them to Christ. Galatia was a region in Asia Minor where the churches of Lystra, Iconium, Antioch, and Derbe (among others) were located.

While in ministry in Antioch Paul was mightily used by the Lord and healed a man who had been crippled since birth. When the Galatian people saw this, they were blown away! They immediately attempted to worship Paul and Barnabas. These poor misguided folks thought the apostles were their gods Jupiter and Mercury! They even wanted to make sacrifices before them. Of course, Paul and Barnabas refused to allow them to do this. Their reaction to this attempt to exalt them rather than God was immediate and heartfelt.

> But when the apostles Barnabas and Paul heard this, they tore their clothes and ran in among the multitude, crying out and saying, "Men, why are you doing these things? We also are men with the same nature as you, and preach to you that you should turn from these useless things to the living God, who made the heaven, the earth, the sea, and all things that are in them."
>
> —ACTS 14:14–15

I love the fact that Paul and Barnabas refused to allow themselves to placed on a pedestal. They were instantly committed to making sure that God got the praise for this mighty miracle. The true test of any man or woman of God is their willingness to give the Lord all the glory and receive none unto themselves. I have been in or around the work of the Lord my entire life. Many times through the years I have personally seen the miraculous manifest in the midst of men, and it is always awesome. I have come to this conclusion, however: miracles and wonders alone don't impress me as much anymore. The real impact is made by who gets the glory.

> Anytime we exalt the men of God above the
> God of men, the church has been charmed.

Paul was unwilling to take any of the glory for himself. Through his faithfulness and humility the pagans of Galatia were soon won over to the real miracle worker, Jesus Christ. In denying any attempt of the Galatian people to exalt them, Paul and Barnabus resisted one of the primary tactics that Satan uses to render the church spellbound.

CHURCH CHARM #1:
HONORING MEN ABOVE GOD

Anytime we exalt the men of God above the God of men, the church has been charmed. I thoroughly and wholeheartedly believe in honoring deserving men and women of God. This is right and well pleasing in the sight of the Lord. Paul instructs us in the Book of Romans to give honor where honor is due. Quite honestly, honor is a rare commodity in many Christian circles nowadays. We would do well if we practiced giving honor to those who merit it more. But trouble is on the horizon when we exalt our leaders as if they are

God's and give glory to them that is due the Lord. Men can and should be honored, but they must never be worshipped.

When men are worshipped, people blindly follow a minister. If the minister does not walk in humility and stop people from exalting him, it becomes truly a case of the blind leading the blind. Only those blind to reality would allow themselves to be worshipped. We must never allow the praise of others to blind us of who we really are.

Paul and Barnabus immediately cried out for the people not to worship them. Do you know why they reacted so desperately and intensely? They did so because they knew who they were and what they had the ability to become without the Lord. They understood that if God abandoned them, they were through. Even in today's church when pride walks in, God walks out.

The church is spellbound when she holds her leadership to no biblical standard of behavior. When people are so taken by the gifting of the minister that they lose sight of the One who gave the minister the gift to begin with, they've been charmed. The ruler, pastor, bishop, or church leader who does not operate in submission to God and His Word is an illegitimate leader. It doesn't matter how smooth or gifted an orator the preacher is, or how great he or she is in ministry, all must be held to the standard of God's Word.

Ministers are not worthy of our worship. The church is charmed when it falls deeper in love with the messenger than the message.

Paul was a man who embraced the tranquility of humility. He had incredible peace in knowing who he had become in the Lord. He was so busy exalting this Jesus who had transformed his life, he had no time or desire to exalt himself. The message he brought to the people of that region was simple and pure. It revolved around one central theme: grace.

Paul's precious preaching stood in total opposition to everything the Galatians had been raised to believe. These people had been bound up their entire lives by the shackles of paganism. Their rituals and heathen festivals dominated their very existence. As much as one-third of their calendar days had been reserved for worshipping, sacrificing to, and reverencing their false gods. The weight of their religion hung around their necks and choked the very life out of them. It must have been an arduous existence as they desperately attempted to fulfill every pagan prerequisite of the day.

> Ministers are not worthy of our worship.
> The church is charmed when it falls deeper in
> love with the messenger than the message.

No matter what they did for their gods, there was always more to do. No matter what they presented to their false deities, they were constantly implored to bring more. There was always another sacrifice, another festival, another demand, or another ritual. In all their striving they were never granted peace or resolve; they could never do enough to satisfy their nonexistent taskmasters.

Into this atmosphere of never-ending, never-satisfying paganism arises a man with a new message—a message that spoke of a savior named Jesus. Can you imagine how amazed these people must have been as they heard the message of Christ and His death on the cross? A message that said, "You don't have to sacrifice to Me; I was sacrificed for you." The message of the cross was life transforming to these desperate people. For the first time ever they heard a message revolving around what their God had already done for them instead of what they should do for their gods.

The gospel must have seemed like a deluge of refreshing cold water in a dry and thirsty desert. Grace, what a concept! Grace whispered into all the unending ritualism and said, "It isn't what you can do; it's what Jesus has done!" I can only imagine the relief and tears of joy as they began to grasp the concept of the incredible love of Jesus.

Even now, reacquaint yourself with the grace of Jesus in your life.

Break every spell of striving off of yourself, and rest in the beauty of what Jesus has done, not in the futility of what you can do.

CHURCH CHARM #2:
BELIEVING YOU CAN EARN GOD'S GRACE

For an incredible season these Galatian believers operated in such grace and liberty, but somewhere along the line they lost their way. They were deceived by false teachers and took their eyes off of grace.

The church that believes the rigors of religion will give them access to the grace of God is a church that has been charmed. The religious spirit is one of the hardest spirits to deal with, and this is exactly what rushed in and charmed the Galatian churches.

After Paul had left Galatia, there was a group of false teachers who invaded these young churches and infiltrated the minds of the people with false teaching. These people were called Judaizers. They came in teaching that the work of Christ was not adequate alone to merit the grace of God...that in order for the Galatians to have liberty and access to God, they would be required to fulfill the religious traditions of Judaism. Sadly these vulnerable new believers fell for this false teaching hook, line, and sinker. Paul said something so striking in Galatians 4. Listen very closely to his words.

> I am afraid for you, lest I have labored for you in vain.
> —GALATIANS 4:11

He told the people he feared for them. Wow! How could fearless Paul, who endured hardship after hardship, abuse after abuse, and beating after beating for the cause of Christ, be afraid? Let me bring clarity to this scripture. Paul didn't have any fear of them or any fear of the devil. He feared for the people because he knew firsthand the power of a religious spirit.

He knew this because prior to his conversion to Christ, he was one of the most devout and religious bigots who had ever lived. He had a comprehension of what it took to be delivered from a religious mind-set. Once a religious spirit sinks its claws into someone, only the power of God can set him free. Paul had spent most of his life spellbound and enslaved to the power of empty religion, and now he saw it invading the lives of those for whom he cared so deeply.

In an act of desperate love he asked the question:

> Oh, foolish Galatians! What magician has hypnotized you and cast an evil spell upon you? For you used to see the meaning of Jesus Christ's death as clearly as though I had waved a placard before you with a picture on it of Christ dying on the cross.
> —GALATIANS 3:1, TLB

He wanted to know what had happened. The understanding they had of the significance of grace and the meaning of the cross was undeniable.

These poor, vulnerable converts had been charmed by the spirit of religion. The spirit of religion is perhaps the most toxic and deadly spirit that assaults the body of Christ even today. It tries to replace the work of Christ with the work of man. By trading paganism for the Judaizers' brand of polluted Christianity, in essence they had exchanged one empty religion for another. It was a sad situation, because the devil cast a spell on them using the power of religion.

Remember, they had spent their entire lives in bondage to rituals and functions. When these Judaizers arrived and said, "You must do all these religious things to know God's grace," the devil hit them right in their most vulnerable place. They returned blindly to what they had been set free from.

It pays to remain aware of Satan's ways; he is a master of deception. Through these false teachers he convinced this church to believe a lie: that Jesus saves but not Jesus alone. Their brand of theology declared, "Jesus saves *comma*," rather than, "Jesus saves *period*." Satan convinced the new converts of Galatia that Jesus plus their religion saved—Jesus plus circumcision, Jesus plus keeping the feast days, Jesus plus keeping their dietary laws, Jesus plus Judaism was the only way to salvation.

Unfortunately these folks left the gospel of grace for the wretchedness of a man-made religion. They had been charmed and immediately began again trying to earn something unobtainable by works.

Grace is never accessed through works; if it were, it would not be grace. The grace of God is accessed only one way—through faith!

> For it is by grace you have been saved, through faith—
> and this not from yourselves, it is the gift of God—not
> by works, so that no one can boast.
> —EPHESIANS 2:8–9, NIV

Putting our faith in anything we do cannot save us. Salvation comes when we put our faith in what Jesus did for us when He gave His life for us on the cross. We take every bit of our faith, and we place that faith in Jesus. When we do this, we come to understand God's grace is the ultimate gift. Something very powerful occurs when this happens; there is absolutely no room for boasting. All we can do then is humbly praise our precious Jesus and lay our worship at His nail-scarred feet.

Today there are many in sacred circles who have been "church charmed" by the devil. They believe that Jesus saves, but not Jesus alone. They will tell you that Jesus saves, plus their religion. Jesus saves, plus their denomination. Jesus saves, plus acting like them. Jesus saves, plus dressing like them. Jesus saves, plus joining their church. Jesus saves *comma*, but as you read this book, be aware of this fact, Jesus saves *period*! The rigors of religion fall shockingly short of ever being able to obtain salvation.

CHURCH CHARM #3:
OPINIONS OF MAN OVER THE AGENDA OF GOD

This church charm creates one of the saddest places in the world. This church is controlled by man's opinion rather than heaven's agenda. The church that is opinion driven has a pronounced air of legalism. Religious opinion trumps everything in the house, even grace. In their spellbound minds nothing is more important than their religious opinion. Their mentality is: you must sing the songs I like, you must preach what I want to hear, you must look how I want you to look, and you must fit into my box. If you do these things, there's room at the cross for you. If you don't do them, there's a "no vacancy" sign where a welcome mat should be.

Paul understood that there would be those in the region of Galatia who would never measure up to the religious ideal of the Judaizers. They would feel unwelcome and unwanted in the Galatian churches, and the kingdom would suffer. Even today it is often that atmosphere that keeps people out of our churches.

Make no mistake about it; the devil gains more lost and hurting souls every time the atmosphere of the church is cold, exclusive, judgmental, and unwelcoming. If the lost are not accepted in the church, where can they go? They feel accepted in the club, the crack house, and the darkness of sin. Satan will always open his arms wide to the struggling. He will roll out the red carpet for the searching and provide a place for the outcast. The devil is often much more committed to the lost than the church is. Never forget: no matter what lost people look like, regardless of what they're grappling with, they must feel accepted in our churches. I've sometimes heard this expressed as "People can belong before they believe."

There is great power in being accepted even when your behavior is unacceptable. I'll share this little story to help explain my point.

When I was a child growing up, we had a special set of clothes reserved only for church. These were our "Sunday clothes." I can remember leaving the house and hearing these strict instructions: "Don't mess up your Sunday clothes."

This was long before any kind of handheld electronic games were around like the ones our kids play with today. Back in those days we played great games after church such as Red Rover and freeze tag. I'd often get caught up in playing with my friends and forget all about my Sunday clothes. I would throw caution to the wind, slide into base, trip and fall, and you guessed it: my Sunday clothes got wrecked. My first thought when this happened was, "Uh-oh, I am in trouble!"

However, when I got home and my parents noticed me, they didn't kick me out of the family or not allow me in the house because of my stains. Why? Because there was a place for me in that house. And even though my behavior was unacceptable, I was still accepted, stains and all.

Churches that will rise up and accept people, stains and all, are actually behaving the most like Jesus. People must know that even if their behavior is unacceptable, they are still accepted. They need to encounter the stain-removing power of the blood of Jesus Christ.

When church-charmed people become stubborn, hardheaded, immovable, and opinionated (as these Judaizers were in Paul's day), they have replaced God's grace with their opinion, and that's idolatry. (See 1 Samuel 15:23.) They are worshipping at the altar of self, and they are spellbound. When they get to the place where no one is able to tell them anything, they're in trouble! When their religious opinion is all that matters, they have made gods of themselves and have been effectively bewitched.

Can I set somebody free? Everybody's not just dying to hear our opinion about everything. Every song, every sermon, every issue, and every outfit does not need to be judged in every church service by everybody. We must replace man's opinion with God's agenda—and God's agenda is saving the lost.

Now fasten your seat belts, because we are about to kick this chapter into overdrive!

CHURCH CHARM #4:
NO NEED TO CHANGE

A charmed church feels no need for modification in their lifestyle and practices and no motivation to work for God. Now let me qualify this statement: I believe in the power of God to change our behavior. I believe in living a life that lines up with the Word of God, not with man-made religious rules. I am fully committed to the fact that when Jesus truly reigns in our own personal world, we will live in a way that reflects our commitment to Him, and the change He has made in our lives will be evident. Our lifestyle will be modified and transformed, but we are not saved by a change in behavior or practice.

We are not saved by our works or because we follow some list of dos and don'ts. According to Paul we are saved by grace and through faith. We place our faith in God's grace. His grace is the only thing that will unlock the precious door of salvation in our lives.

> You are not God's afterthought, mistake, or one
> He just can't find a place for in the kingdom.

Faith and grace are the essentials of being born again, but there is more to our walk with God than just salvation. We are saved *by* grace, *through* faith, and (get ready for this) *for* works. Look again at Ephesians 2, and let's add verse 10 into the mix.

> For it is *by grace* you have been saved, *through faith*—and this not from yourselves, it is the gift of God—not by works, so that no one can boast. For we are God's workmanship, created in Christ Jesus *to do good works,* which God prepared in advance for us to do.
> —EPHESIANS 2:8–10, NIV, EMPHASIS ADDED

Do you see the three steps in these three verses? We are saved by grace, through faith, and for works. Redeemed and saved by the precious blood of Jesus is what we are; work is what we do. God saved us because He loves us, but also because He desires to use us.

You should stop and think about that for just a moment. The God of the universe finds you useful and necessary. You are not God's afterthought, mistake, or one He just can't find a place for in the kingdom. On the contrary, your destiny in God makes you a kingdom asset. Even when you feel unfruitful and inadequate, God sees you as a person of purpose that He can mightily use for His own glory.

One of the greatest tragedies in the world is when the church is charmed by the enemy into doing nothing significant for the cause of Christ. The hope of the earth is the church operating at its full potential—fully alive, fully awake, and fully aware of a world in desperate need of our gospel of hope.

I looked up several different secular sources to define the word *church*. Virtually everyone defined the church as a building where religious services were held. That may be the secular view of the church, and unfortunately, to a great degree, that is the church's view of itself. But it certainly isn't the Lord's view of His church.

In the New Testament the word *church* is translated from the Greek word *ekklesia*, which means the called-out ones. In the early days of Christianity there were no beautiful cathedrals or large houses built for worship. The church was not known for where they worshipped; they were known for who they were, and they were the called-out ones. They grew the church by being salt and light outside of religious buildings.

As I write this book, we have just completed construction on our new worship center. It's the largest place of worship in Central Florida. We can accommodate thousands of people. As thankful as we are for this building, it is only a building; it's not the church. There is not a cathedral, building, or even a stadium that could be erected that would be able to contain the church, because the church is not a building made with human hands. The church is the called-out ones bought by the precious blood of Jesus.

> We often equate unity with sameness. Unity is not sameness; unity is oneness in purpose. It's different people headed the same direction.

When the Lord sees His church, He doesn't see us by our divisions. He doesn't see the Baptist church, Methodist church, Pentecostal church, or anything else. He does not see a black church, a white church, a Hispanic church, or any other racial division. The only things the Lord sees are the called-out ones! God doesn't see buildings; God sees believers!

This is why it is more important than ever that the called-out ones be in unity. The problem is, we often equate unity with sameness. Unity is not sameness; unity is oneness in purpose. It's different people headed in the same direction. A football team is not unified because everyone plays the same position; that's uniformity. A football team is unified because everyone is headed for the same goal. Every player knows he cannot get there alone. As the *ekklesia* of the Lord, in our diversity we must never forget we are headed for the same goal. And we cannot achieve that goal alone.

CHURCH CHARM #5:
COMPETITION BETWEEN CHURCHES

Churches must complete; they must never compete. Charmed churches compete with each other. Often what we see as building the church, God sees as relocating the church. We are called to do more than swap people; we are called to build the church and enlarge it by creating new disciples for Christ.

The church has been *called* out, and we must *get* out if we are to *bring others* out. Satan trembles every time church people recognize their mission. Our mission is not to *go* to church; our mission is to *be* the church. The church is saved by grace, through faith, and for works. The church is a working, moving, called-out, functioning body, full of faith, grace, and works! The church that is not making an impact outside its walls has been charmed.

I will explain what it means to be called out by using a surprising Old Testament example. Most of us remember the story of Moses. Moses is known as the deliverer of God's people. He led them out of the bondage of Egyptian slavery and captivity. The chronicle of his life is amazing.

> Our mission is not to *go* to church;
> our mission is to *be* the church.

In the days of Moses the people of God had multiplied and grown even while in captivity to their Egyptian tormentors. They grew so much that Pharaoh became afraid and threatened by them and issued a decree that all the Hebrew male babies born should be put to death. Moses was born with great destiny during this window of time, but he arrived with a death sentence hanging over his head.

Anytime there is great potential for kingdom purpose, the devil will do all he can to kill it. His attack is not always about where you are; sometimes his attack is against where he sees your potential taking you. It is an attack against your destiny. He sees the potential of where you're headed and what you can become, and Satan is afraid of you just as Pharaoh was afraid of Moses.

There are some powerful things that struck me revolving around the life of this mighty world changer named Moses. In this chaotic atmosphere Moses should have never lived. But his mother saw him as a child born with purpose.

When she saw him that he was a goodly child...
—Exodus 2:2, KJV

The Hebrew word *towb*, translated as the English word *goodly*, is a very beautiful word. In the original language of the Old Testament it means valuable in estimation. Moses's mother looked at him, and the destiny that had been deposited into him spoke to her. His destiny spoke when he wasn't capable of saying a word. He didn't even know who he was at that immature place in his life. She saw something in him he could not even see in himself! It was as if she looked at this baby and said, "There is just something about you. You have been born with a purpose." She recognized that there was a divinely deposited destiny in this child.

"There Is Just Something About You"

I believe this with all my heart: in the same way that Moses was born with a great destiny and assignment, we who have been born again by grace and through faith have a great destiny and assignment in and over our lives. The devil does not want us to see it; in fact, he is doing everything he can to abort it.

As a born-again believer, there is just something about you. The devil would like to defeat you, but you have a purpose in God, and He has a plan for you. If the devil could have destroyed you, you would have been destroyed a long time ago. Don't lose sight of why you have been born again. You have a divine assignment as part of the church. God wants to use you because you are *goodly*; you are valuable in estimation. You are a person of potential!

We must not allow ourselves to be church charmed. Many in the church are deeply under a spell. To them church has become a place where religious people who have similar views gather. It is where we have majored in the minors and minored in the majors. There is more concern about bake sales, fashion trends, the latest gossip, and aspiration for position than anything else.

Many in the church are drunk on their titles while a world perishes without the gospel. In their communities, though they have been gathering for many years, the poor remain poor, the hungry remain hungry, and the lost remain lost. Why? All because the church charmer is on the loose, and he's doing a great job. These religious gatherings often become board driven instead of vision led. My prayer is that the same power that shook the Upper Room would shake the church boardroom!

You must never allow yourself to be church charmed. God has brought you through all that He has brought you through because He has plans for you. I've heard it said this way: "God gets it *to* you so He can get it *through* you." If God has given you victory over sins, helped you through a trial, healed you from an illness, or blessed you in any number of ways, He has done it so that He can use you to help others experience the same things.

Moses had to go through peril, but God had a purpose for his life. I have had my share of peril, and I am sure you probably have as well. In fact, you may be facing peril right now, but never forget this: your purpose is greater than your peril. Anytime there is great destiny in your life, you must not be surprised by great attack.

There are seasons in life when it seems like all hell is against us. That was certainly true as it relates to Moses. His attack was not about where he was at the time; he was a baby and was no threat to anyone. Moses's attack was over where he was going and what he was to accomplish for God.

In the same way the attack of the enemy against your life is not for where you are now but for where you are going. There was great destiny locked inside that baby named Moses, and the desire of the enemy was to kill the baby's destiny! And there is great destiny locked in you! But you cannot afford to become overwhelmed by Satan's attack.

Your destiny in God can cause you to have to endure seasons of intense attack. At times you are literally enduring an assault on what God has divinely deposited in you. We see this example time and again in the Word of God. Just look at Daniel in the den of hungry lions; Shadrach, Meshach, and Abednego in the fire seven times hotter than normal; David being pursued by Saul; and John on Patmos. But no matter what you are going through, don't be mesmerized, hypnotized, or spellbound by your trouble.

> By faith Moses' parents hid him for three months after
> he was born, because they saw he was no ordinary child.
> —HEBREWS 11:23, NIV

I declare this over every person reading this book right now, "You are no ordinary child; *you are a child of the King!* You are an extraordinary person, and you have an extraordinary purpose." When you have extraordinary destiny, don't be surprised by extraordinary attack. But there is something mighty that must be realized by extraordinary people who endure extraordinary attack. They should expect extraordinary deliverance! Expect God to come through!

God will use what we see as senseless seasons to expose His plan in our lives. There is a verse in the story of Moses that is so powerful to me.

> But when she could no longer hide him...
> —EXODUS 2:3

We all go through times in our lives when we feel like we are hidden. If we are not careful, the devil will cast a spell on us and convince us that because it's not time yet for us to be fully used in our destiny for God, it will never be time.

Have you ever felt like there was great destiny in you, but your situation kept you in a place where it seemed you were in "park" rather than "drive"? Moses was hidden away; a mighty deliverer was hidden away. But while he was hidden, it was not in vain; he was growing! At times God will keep you in a season in your life that may challenge you. Don't let it get you down.

Whether you realize it or not, God knows, people around you know, and Satan knows this fact: you are growing.

Sometimes the pains we feel in the season we are in are actually growing pains! All through his life Moses endured pain, and the devil would have loved to cast a spell on him and paralyze him in his pain. The pain was just preparation for his purpose.

On some level you may be in pain right now, but the pain you're going through is just preparation for your destiny! That's why you can't afford to get mad and bitter at people who have hurt you. Even in Christian circles I have seen people so wounded through church hurt that they become church charmed by the enemy. They come to services, sit through sermons, and all the while they are hiding their wounds. They are mesmerized by their misery and hypnotized by their hurt. They feel too broken for a breakthrough and too wounded to work. Hell's spells are active and alive in the lives of people who carry all this pain.

But don't forget how and why we are saved: *by grace, through faith,* and *for works.*

Even the pain we have endured has only prepared us for the destiny God has called us to walk in! Don't allow the devil to cast a spell on you. When you go through hard times, you will make it by grace, through faith, and for works.

WHEN YOU COME OUT, BRING SOMEBODY WITH YOU!

We have already established that the church is the *ekklesia*, the called-out ones, and that the church is not a building but a people. We have been called out of sin, called out of darkness, and called out of bondage. We have been called out for a reason and a purpose. When we were saved, we were enlisted into the greatest plan of all, the cause of the church. We have been saved to and for works. We have been saved that we might glorify God and that we might spread the power of this precious gospel.

I want you to fast-forward with me in the theater of your mind from Moses's birth all the way to when Moses had his glorious encounter with the Lord at the burning bush in the desert. At this stage of life he is now eighty years old. He spent forty years in Egypt and forty years in the dessert. In Exodus 3 the Bible says that the Lord called to Moses, and in those few moments his life changed forever. It was on the backside of the desert that Moses received his assignment.

> And the LORD said: "I have surely seen the oppression of My people who are in Egypt, and have heard their cry because of their taskmasters, for I know their sorrows. So I have come down to deliver them out of the hand of the Egyptians, and to bring them up from that land to a good and large land, to a land flowing with milk and honey, to the place of the Canaanites and the Hittites and the Amorites and the Perizzites and the Hivites and the Jebusites. Now therefore, behold, the cry of the children of Israel has come to Me, and I have also seen the oppression with which the Egyptians oppress them. Come now, therefore, and I will send you to Pharaoh that you may bring My people, the children of Israel, out of Egypt."
> —EXODUS 3:7–10

Moses was eighty years old, he had been in the desert for forty years, and I am sure in the natural he may have resigned himself to the fact that he would die in the desert. But at eighty God spoke to him and said, "Man, I'm going to use you!"

Some people get caught in the desert and think they can never come out. The enemy has charmed them, and they believe that they can never escape the dry place. These thirsty souls have been literally placed under a spell, and Satan has convinced them that they are no use to God and His plan.

In essence God said to Moses, "I have laid My hand on you

to bring out the children of Israel." As we peruse this chapter, it's obvious that Moses struggled with doubt. He doubted himself, and he doubted his destiny. The desert was the only reality he could grasp. How could God use him, he wondered. He told God of his issues (as if God didn't already know) and his shortcomings. I can hear him: "Lord, I st-st-st-stutter; nobody will believe me; it just cannot work!" He had many excuses, but his excuses did not negate or lessen God's call on his life.

Moses had the hand of the Lord on his life when he was just a baby, and the Lord had His hand on Moses right there in the desert. God told Moses that He wanted him to bring His people out. And if anyone knew about being brought out, it was Moses.

> And the child grew, and she brought him to Pharaoh's daughter, and he became her son. So she called his name Moses, saying, "Because I drew him out of the water."
> —Exodus 2:10

When Pharaoh's daughter named the baby Moses, she didn't know that she was pointing that child toward his destiny. The name *Moses* means pulled or brought out. She named him this because she brought him out of the river Nile.

Look at the life of Moses. I want you to see how God was preparing this boy named "brought out." He had spent his life being brought out. He was brought out from his family and placed in a basket to float down the river. He was brought out of that river through the divine hand of the Lord. He wound up being brought out of the palace and fleeing to the desert. He was now about to be brought out of the desert and into Egypt to deliver the Israelites.

His whole life he had lived the process of being brought out. And now at eighty years old, standing at that burning bush in the holy presence of God, he must have had an epiphany. All those years he had spent being brought out had been for a purpose and a reason. He may have even understood how his name connected to his destiny! Moses. Brought out. It all started making sense. He had been brought out because his destiny was to bring others out!

So God took him through what seemed like a grueling and intense process, but there was purpose in the process. How can you bring someone else out if you have never been brought out yourself?

God brings us out in order that we might be able to bring someone else out with us! Moses could do the work of a deliverer because he had been delivered himself! Can you imagine? As Moses stood there hearing from God Himself relative to his destiny, suddenly every hard place that he had ever walked started making sense. All the tough times, the heartaches, the long days, and the lonely nights finally came together. He had been brought out to bring others out!

And as you read this book, if you are a part of the *ekklesia*, the called-out ones, you have been called out for a purpose. Just as Moses was brought out, you have been brought out. You had to walk where you walked and go through what you went through so God could use you to bring somebody else out.

God has saved you by grace, through faith, and for works. He called you out, but it's not enough for you to come out alone. As the called-out ones we are now given the high call of calling others out. That is what the church is to do; when we come out, we are to bring others out with us. Don't come out alone! As the called-out ones and the brought-out ones, we must bring others out.

Many sit in sanctuaries service after service; they are good people, but they are church charmed. The devil has them convinced that going to church is all there is, that somehow gathering in a building is enough—but it's not enough. We have been brought out to work for the Lord. It is good to come out, but real victory is bringing somebody with you!

Don't let the devil charm you into ineffectiveness because of the blemishes of your past or the inadequacies of your present. God knows our struggles, but He has chosen each of us anyhow. The called-out ones must call out others. Satan trembles at the thought of the body of Christ recognizing its assignment and calling a lost world into the love of Jesus.

A GOSPEL STRONG ENOUGH
TO SAVE THE WORLD

Paul asked the church in Galatia, "Who bewitched you?" He saw that they were under a spell and wanted to shake them from their trance.

The word *bewitched* is an intense word with several layers of meaning. Here at the last of this chapter I want to touch on the part of this word that means to fascinate and please to such a degree as to take away the power of resistance.

One of the ways the enemy effectively charms the church is when we allow him to infiltrate our ranks, to fascinate and please us to such a degree that we no longer resist him. It is very important to note this fact: there can be no revival without resistance.

It is sad to admit, but much of this world has plunged itself into an abyss of immorality and unrighteousness. And quite honestly, to acknowledge our societal struggles in any way often causes us to be labeled intolerant and insensitive. The confronting message of the cross is becoming passé, unacceptable, and politically incorrect. In an effort to become more embraceable to everyone, many Christian organizations have lost their power to influence anyone, all because they have diluted the message. A diluted gospel is a polluted gospel, and a polluted gospel is no gospel at all.

In this X-rated world there is a decaffeinated gospel on the rise.

Coffee goes through an intense process to be decaffeinated. First, unroasted green coffee beans are steamed. Then they are rinsed with a solvent that removes the caffeine from the beans. The process is repeated eight to twelve times until 97 percent of the caffeine is removed and its effects are diminished.[1]

There are several effects that caffeine has on the body, including stimulating your heart, respiratory, and nervous systems. It causes messages to be sent across your nervous system more quickly. Caffeine stimulates the cortex of your brain, heightening the intensity of brain activity. Caffeine aids in keeping you awake and alert for a period of time. I realize that too much caffeine is not good for you, but here is the point. Most of us get the majority of our caffeine from drinking coffee. Once it is decaffeinated, all of its influence over the mind and body is gone.

It's the same with a decaffeinated church; when we continuously water down and dilute our message, it loses its power and effectiveness. We lose our edge, and church becomes a sleepy ritual. We no longer have the power to stimulate hearts and minds for an eternal purpose.

Ironically as I am writing this chapter, I am staying in a hotel in Phoenix, Arizona. My room has a coffeemaker in it. Beside the coffeemaker there sits a little sign describing that the coffee the hotel provides helps to support coffee growers who are committed to preserving the rain forests. Because of their support of the preservation of the rain forest, in big bold letters on the little sign are these words: "Coffee Strong Enough to Save the World."

That is powerful to me, because of where I am in this chapter. There is only one gospel strong enough to change the world, and that's an undiluted gospel.

I certainly believe that our church gatherings should be bathed in unconditional love and hope. We have already established that everyone should feel accepted. But there must be truth spoken in the atmosphere of love. Where there is a lack of truth, there will always be a lack of love. We help no one struggling with sin and bondage of any kind unless we teach the power of a cross that delivers from every kind of sin and bondage.

Satan has cast a spell on many in the church, and they are pleased to such a degree that the power of any resistance is gone. So often in our gatherings people are just hearing what they want to hear; they are never challenged, never pressed, and never confronted with the love of Christ to effect change in their lives. Often we never hear of our responsibility to others.

A charmed church is teeming with unbelieving believers. Unbelieving believers don't want to speak out; they would rather just blend in. They don't want to truly take God at His Word and become a doer of that Word rather than just a hearer only. Bottom line, they just don't want to rock the boat. Jesus never called Peter to rock the boat; He called him to get out of the boat! And as the *ekklesia* we are called to take this message out of our sanctuaries. But there must be a message to take out!

Satan has effectively charmed many in the church until we are satisfied to remain muted, quiet, and pathetically afraid. We have megachurches (I love them and am blessed to pastor one), but many of them have been charmed. If we are not about loving and winning the lost and discipling people, we have been effectively charmed. It doesn't matter how incredibly we do other things; if we fail to do these essentials, Satan has us under a spell. A megachurch without a mega cause will turn into a mega mess.

Anytime we lose sight of our assignment to the lost and hurting and stop resisting Satan, we are no use to heaven and no bother to hell. We can have great music, awesome programs, and creative services and still be a joke in hell. Only when we remain radically committed to the truth of God's Word and the mission of God's heart do we worry hell.

This lonely, hurting world needs so much more than a decaffeinated church. Those who are bound and blind are desperate to hear a bondage-breaking, sight-giving gospel. Our gatherings must be dripping in the tangible love of Jesus, and our lives must be as well. Our gospel is a "whosoever will let them come" gospel, and when they come, may they experience love like never before.

When we address the hard issues, we must address them in love, never backing up one millimeter from truth, totally caffeinated and radically committed to sharing the grace of Jesus. Jesus forgives, Jesus loves, and Jesus restores. When we apply this philosophy to our gatherings, church charm is destroyed, Satan is defeated, and Jesus is exalted.

As a called-out one, commit yourself as never before to calling others out. The church must resist every attempt of the devil to charm us and place us under any spell through his deceptive ways.

You are in the kingdom to make a difference, and as you walk in clarity and liberty, you will! Declare this right now over your life: "I am saved by grace, through faith, and for works."

Chapter 6

The JEZEBEL SPELL

ONE OF THE MOST DOMINATING AND CONTROLLING spirits unleashed against the church and the people of God is the spirit of Jezebel. Jezebel was an actual Old Testament character who lived in the ninth century B.C. Her story is told in the books of 1 and 2 Kings. And then her name is never mentioned again in the Bible until about nine hundred years later in the Book of Revelation, where it is spoken by Jesus Himself.

> Nevertheless, I have this against you: You tolerate that woman Jezebel, who calls herself a prophetess. By her teaching she misleads my servants into sexual immorality and the eating of food sacrificed to idols. I have given her time to repent of her immorality, but she is unwilling. So I will cast her on a bed of suffering, and I will make those who commit adultery with her suffer intensely, unless they repent of her ways. I will strike her children dead. Then all the churches will know that I am he who searches hearts and minds, and I will repay each of you according to your deeds.
> —REVELATION 2:20–23, NIV

In the Old Testament Jezebel lives and breathes, but in the New Testament she represents a spirit. In the Old Testament Jezebel was the wife of King Ahab of Israel. She was not a Jew; this marriage was actually a political marriage that was designed to strengthen

Israel's alliance with the Phoenicians. It afforded Jews the opportunity to make use of the great ports of Sidon and Tyre in order to strengthen their ability to trade with other countries. This so-called alliance proved to be disastrous for both Israel and Ahab.

> And as if it had been a light thing for him to walk in the sins of Jeroboam the son of Nebat, he took for his wife Jezebel the daughter of Ethbaal king of the Sidonians, and went and served Baal and worshiped him.
>
> —1 KINGS 16:31, ESV

Her arrival in Israel was more like an invasion. She didn't invade militarily but spiritually. Ahab was a weak-kneed leader with no real conviction for Jehovah God. The Bible says that Ahab went and worshipped Baal. Jezebel brought her idolatry with her, and it exploded throughout the Northern Kingdom of Israel. She worshipped Baal and Astheroth. Ahab found her impossible to resist, and though he was the king and wore the crown, she was the boss and wore the pants.

Jezebel only gained access to the kingdom because Ahab invited her in. Even though this marriage was strictly forbidden by Mosaic law, Ahab disregarded what he knew was right and married her anyway. She came in because she was allowed in. In our churches and our lives, Satan will always quickly come in wherever he is allowed access. But Satan can never take control; it must be yielded to him. *Do not yield.* Do what Ahab refused to do and honor the Word of God, and you will deny the devil access.

Jezebel's father's name was Ethbaal, which means "with Baal." Without a doubt Ethbaal was with Baal, and he raised a daughter who was radically with Baal. As weak-willed as Ahab was for Jehovah, Jezebel was strong-willed for Baal.

Several statements made in the Old Testament book of 1 Kings reveal Jezebel's place and position of satanic control in Israel. It's important to understand the behavior of Jezebel as recorded in the

Old Testament because it will provide great insight into why, in the New Testament, God called the spirit unleashed against Thyatira "the spirit of Jezebel."

THE FEAR FACTOR

> For so it was, while Jezebel massacred the prophets of the LORD, that Obadiah had taken one hundred prophets and hidden them, fifty to a cave, and had fed them with bread and water.
> —1 KINGS 18:4

Pay close attention to those words. It was Jezebel who massacred the prophets of the Lord. It was at her command that the prophets of God were removed from Israel. She either had them exiled or put to death.

God's prophets represented the voice of the Lord to His people. Jezebel was driven to silence that voice of God by any and all means necessary.

Jezebel ruled and controlled through intimidation and fear. Intimidation was definitely the weapon she wielded, and it became a great factor in instilling fear in the hearts and minds of the people, even in the leaders of God. Her intimidation was so thorough and intense that she even intimidated the prophet Elisha for a season.

Fast-forward nineteen hundred years later to Thyatira, and we find the Lord issuing this indictment against this church.

> Nevertheless, I have this against you: You tolerate that woman Jezebel...
> —REVELATION 2:20, NIV

The agenda of the spirit of Jezebel in the New Testament is the same as the agenda of the real Jezebel in the Old Testament. Jezebel wants to silence the voice of the Lord. She will do everything she can do to silence the voice of the Lord to His people. We must not deceive ourselves; the spirit of Jezebel is alive and well in the world today. Her most despised foe is the pastor, prophet, or any spiritual leader sensitive to the voice of the Lord.

You can always spot the spirit of Jezebel working in the church when certain people rise up and become critical of God's ordained leaders. Jezebel in the church is all about control. She nags, fusses, gripes, complains, and attacks the spiritual authority of the ministry. Just as Jezebel of old dominated and controlled Ahab, the spirit of Jezebel wants to dominate God's ordained leadership in the church.

Ahab was Jezebel's pawn that she moved and manipulated to serve her own corrupt agenda. And it's the same way in the church; those dominated by the spirit of Jezebel do not want a pastor—they want a puppet. Jezebel's goal is to destroy anointed leaders and replace them with those whom she can dominate.

Very often the spirit of Jezebel will show up in leadership in the church. They wind up ruling the house even though they don't have the title or authority to do so. Jezebel is working when a deacon, leader, or even a staff member begins to undermine the authority of God's chosen leader so that they can gain power and influence. Jezebel may seem outwardly gracious, but she is determined to get her way. She will pout, give the silent treatment, flow in self-pity, and act wounded or hurt in order to gain control. She is ruthless and will even use sexuality to try and dominate spiritual leaders.

Just remember, behind that big smile are sharp spiritual teeth just looking for a chance to devour. Jezebel chews spiritual leaders up and spits them out.

Jezebel's name has two meaning. First her name means, "married to Baal." Baal represented opposition to God and His plan in the Old Testament. Very often the people of the Lord fell victim to being drawn into idolatry and immorality. This, of course, was in total opposition to God's plan. The spirit of Jezebel is married to the devil, because she is always in opposition to the plan of God.

You can always recognize the spirit of Jezebel because she will continually oppose the plan of God given to the man of God. Think about the people over the years in your spiritual walk who have exhibited these characteristics. There is a strong possibility that they were manifesting the spirit of Jezebel.

The secondary meaning for the name Jezebel is, "inability to cohabitate." Jezebel cannot get along with anyone in authority because her marriage to the devil forbids it! Be very careful in aligning yourself with people who are in opposition to the man or woman of God.

You may be wondering what to do if the spiritual leader makes decisions that consistently contradict God's Word. This is very easy: pray for that leader, and seek out a new spiritual leader.

Jezebel moves stealthily through the congregation and leadership and does all she can do to silence the voice of God through the man or woman of God in authority in the church. She is good at her job; she is a seductress and is very adept at manipulating the hearts of people.

In Revelation 2:20 Jesus said that she calls herself a prophetess. Now there are a couple of things that must be noticed here. First, she *calls herself* a prophetess. She is not validated, endorsed, or supported by God. Her title is 100 percent self-proclaimed. Secondly, as a so-called prophetess, she is spiritual. But if true prophets of God are led by the Spirit of the Lord, who are false prophets led by? The answer to that question should be quite clear. False prophets are led and inspired by Satan.

As a false prophet Jezebel loves to give false words and has false visions and attempts to come across as extremely spiritual. But don't be fooled; everything this spirit does is to serve her own agenda. She is after one thing, and that's control.

This spirit preys on weak-minded believers and weak leaders. I have dealt with this spirit over the years in my church. Jezebel will often show up where there is prayer, because remember, she wants to disrupt the voice of God to the people of God. The most effective way to get the mind of God and to hear the voice of God is through prayer. So the spirit of Jezebel works hard to sabotage prayer.

Jezebel will often show up where there is prayer, because remember, she wants to disrupt the voice of God to the people of God.

My wife, Dawn, is an incredible intercessor. She hosts and oversees an awesome prayer ministry at our church. Several years ago a person started showing up in these meetings. This individual was very "spiritual" and would begin to walk around our prayer gatherings and pray over people and give false words. The spirit of Jezebel that dominated this individual wanted control of those meetings and was doing everything it could to gain it. The spirit of Jezebel was doing what Jezebel does, becoming a distraction. This spirit had to be dealt with, because if we didn't, we knew the praying people would grow weary of Jezebel's antics and quit coming to pray together at all. If this had happened, in a great way the voice of the Lord could have been hindered and Jezebel would have won.

There was a particular day that Dawn had hosted a prayer meeting, and this person came. At the end of the meeting my wife, who was the legitimate authority over these meetings, dismissed everyone after a powerful time of intercession. Dawn and I were scheduled to speak somewhere that evening and had jumped into our car immediately following this prayer meeting and headed out. While on the way to preach as a guest at another church, the Spirit of the Lord spoke to me to go back to our church. I did, and when my wife and I arrived where the prayer meeting had been held earlier, there this individual stood, dominated and controlled by the spirit of Jezebel.

The people were kneeling at this person's feet. False prophecy was being spoken over each one in the room. I believe the spirit of

Jezebel was more than a little shocked when my wife and I walked back in.

I immediately stood the folks up, prayed over each person, dismissed the meeting, and confronted this person. In Jesus's name I won't be an Ahab!

Not long after that this person left our church, but not before the spirit of Jezebel had bewitched and cast a spell on a couple of our precious people. They were seduced from under God's spiritual covering in their lives and left also. Jezebel looks for the weak ones and preys on them.

CAUSING THE LEGIT TO QUIT

The spirit of Jezebel brings such an attack against spiritual leaders that unless they are strong, they will run from their appointed assigned place. A great example of this is revealed in how Elijah responded to the attack of Jezebel in 1 Kings 19.

> Now Ahab told Jezebel all that Elijah had done, and how he had killed all the prophets with the sword. Then Jezebel sent a messenger to Elijah, saying, "So may the gods do to me and even more, if I do not make your life as the life of one of them by tomorrow about this time." And he was afraid and arose and ran for his life and came to Beersheba, which belongs to Judah, and left his servant there.
> —1 KINGS 19:1–3, NAS

This whole discourse of Scripture is amazing because of the events that had just occurred at the end of chapter 18. Elisha had seen the most important victories in his life. He had just witnessed God's powerful fire fall on the altar before the congregation of Israel. The people fell and worshipped Jehovah, and a horrific drought supernaturally ended because of the favor of God. Four hundred fifty of Baal's prophets had been put to death, and God had used Elisha in an indescribable way.

I have stood on Mt. Carmel in Israel many times and envisioned what it must have been like to witness these awesome events first-hand as they unfolded. There is absolutely no denying the powerful hand of God that rested on this great prophet's life.

He was certainly on spiritual high plane when all this occurred. But in the very next chapter Jezebel finds out about it and sends a messenger to Elisha with these words (and I paraphrase), "You are dead meat, boy!" She didn't even threaten him personally; she sent someone else. It seems to me that Elisha would have said, "Bring it on; I have been waiting for this fight!" After all the victory that God had given him, nothing should have been able to stop him, but it did—or rather *she* did.

Instead of turning and fighting, Elisha turned and fled. He was so debilitated by her threat that he became spiritually disoriented. He somehow lost sight of the greatness of God, fell into depression, and ran for his life. He even prayed and asked God to let him die. He was fleeing when he should have been fighting.

Elijah ran and eventually hid in a cave. He was cut off, isolated, and out of place. In fact, in the cave, the Lord came to him and said, "Elijah, what are you doing here?" It is plain to see that this was not the place that Elijah was supposed to be. Jezebel had isolated him and made him want to quit.

Fear is one of the most powerful weapons the enemy has. Jezebel paralyzed perhaps the greatest Old Testament prophet without ever laying a hand on him. This mighty man, who was full of faith one day, was full of fear the next.

One of the saddest things to see is a spiritual leader who has been "Jezebelled"—leaders who have seen God bring great victories in their lives and ministries but wind up fearfully fleeing when they should be ferociously fighting. The spirit of Jezebel will come against spiritual leaders in such a way that they wind up disoriented, depressed, and isolated. At times like these, leaders can feel alone because Jezebel will do everything in her power to discourage them personally and discredit them publicly.

Elijah quickly lost sight of all that God had done for him. He became convinced that he alone was following God. God spoke to him and told him he had seven thousand who had not bowed a knee to Baal. But until that moment Elijah was convinced he was alone.

The spirit of Jezebel works hard to fill God's spiritual leaders with fear and loneliness. These two conditions account for more ministerial resignations than anything else. Jezebel has an agenda; if she can't rule the leader, she will seek to destroy the leader and replace him with someone she can control.

BACKGROUND OF A BACKSTABBER

Jezebel is the ultimate backstabber because she is about one thing: self-preservation. As you read this, you might wonder what kind of person is vulnerable to being controlled by the Jezebel spirit. The Jezebel spirit often, but not always, manifests in women. One of the main trademarks of the person who allows this spirit to have control is a *massive* ego. A person controlled by Jezebel is driven to seek out positions, titles, and spotlights. Jezebel loves to dominate and feel as if she is the center of attention. She is jealous, critical, and petty if she doesn't get her way.

Individuals who fall prey to being controlled by this spirit have usually (but not always) had issues with submission their entire lives. It didn't just start in church. Very often it has been a reality that they have dealt with even as far back as childhood.

The person who entertains the spirit of Jezebel will come across as extremely confident. More often than not, however, this individual is plagued by insecurities. A discerning leader will see right through their confident veneer and recognize their vulnerability. Jezebel is attracted to people who feel like they have something to prove, and they are driven by inner thoughts and struggles that tell them they are not good enough and don't measure up.

Because of tremendous insecurities these people are easily threatened and extremely territorial. They have usually dealt with some type of rejection in their life that has fueled this toxic behavior. Jezebel preys on people who have hurts in their past that are unhealed. These people have allowed themselves to become infected by bitterness and unforgiveness, and because of this they are extremely vulnerable.

Once these individuals are under Jezebel's control, whatever is in their world has to be under their control. This is the way they find security and purpose. The spirit of Jezebel can affect anyone, but she is especially drawn to those with some or all of these characteristics.

UNCOVER, DISCOVER, RECOVER

The spirit of Jezebel must not be ignored if victory is to be secured. Jezebel must be uncovered, the damage she has inflicted must be discovered, and whatever has been lost must be recovered. Jezebel is determined to have control no matter what the price. Ministries and people mean nothing to her; she only cares about her agenda. Jezebel must be uncovered because she is often covert in her actions.

Jezebel is full of lies and flattery; she will tell you what you want to hear if it serves her purpose. Meanwhile, she will undermine, discredit, and continuously manipulate people by twisting the truth. Jezebel will come across as humble and oftentimes submissive. Even when she seems to be submitting, it is always with the ulterior motive of control. But this reality must not be ignored: Jezebel will surrender or submit to no one.

Remember, her name means inability to cohabitate. The only relationship she is satisfied with is the one she can control. Never think that by giving in even a little bit, Jezebel will be satisfied. No matter how much control she has, she wants more.

Upon evaluation it is easy to discover the places where Jezebel is hiding, because she is almost always hiding in plain sight. Jezebel can sit on the leadership board of the church. Those who have the spirit of Jezebel want to dominate and control how the funds are spent. They view the pastor or spiritual leader as a hireling who works for them. The pastor exists to fulfill their own personal agenda and is truly not their leader; on the contrary, they are his.

My own father dealt with this. My dad pastored his first church when he was seventeen and preached the gospel for fifty-five years. He was a precious pastor and what I call "love on wheels."

Late in his ministry there was a man on his leadership board who wanted him to leave the church. This man sought to control everything. He began to undermine my father and tried to discredit him with the people.

I was grown and gone by this time. I remember coming home one time and talking to Dad during this hard season of his ministry. It seems like yesterday. He looked at me with his sweet old tired blue eyes and began to tell me the story of this board member. I remember his words clearly. "Son," my dad said, "he told me he had his finger on the pulse of the people, and my departure was what they wanted."

One thing cannot be ignored: this man was not the spiritual God-ordained leader in the house. What was he doing with his "finger on the pulse of the people"? Heartbreakingly, not long after that, my dad left. Most of the people exited shortly after that. Chalk one up for Jezebel.

Most often people under Jezebel's influence seek to control the funds because they know whoever controls the money, to a large degree, controls the vision. Entire families can be submitted to the spirit of Jezebel. These folks stay in church leadership almost indefinitely. I have seen one or two families with the spirit of Jezebel hold a church hostage for generations. They don't want a pastor or a leader; they want a figurehead—nothing more, nothing less, and nothing else.

It is a sad day when a board member feels like he knows more about the vision and direction of the church than the God-called, God-ordained leader. Leaders are placed by God over the church and should be allowed to lead in submission to the Lord and the vision God has given them. I'm certainly not advocating that pastors shouldn't remain accountable, but a true leader must lead and chart the course for the ministry. If there is a board member with more power and influence than God's chosen leader in ministry, there is a good chance Jezebel is sitting on the board.

Jezebel wants to control what is taught in the church as well as the moving of the Holy Spirit. She is never satisfied unless you are singing the songs she likes or preaching the messages she wants to hear. She creates an atmosphere of striving in the church rather than peace.

Over the years I have held every position of ministry within the church with the exception of women's director! I started out in youth and music ministry. I personally dealt with people who were determined to control the praise and worship. I tried so very hard to make them happy, but they were only happy if I was singing what they wanted, in the style they wanted, for as long as they wanted. I would strive and stress out trying to please them, but it was impossible. In that season they were in control.

When I operated and flowed in liberty, the majority of the church was ministered to and changed by God's presence. But there were one or two who wanted to control everything that went on during worship and didn't mind vocalizing their displeasure to me and anyone else who would listen. I would watch them during worship sometimes; they looked as if they had been baptized in pickle juice!

It wasn't until I got a little bit older that I understood that many times in dealing with this situation, I had been encountering the spirit of Jezebel. Real breakthrough came when I realized I was not called to *please* people; I was called to *lead* them. My calling was to please God.

I remember being so intimidated and upset in those early years of ministry. I was literally in bondage! Jezebel seeks to bind the leader, because when she binds the leader, she binds the church!

One of the things that Jezebel must have to be successful is an Ahab. Ahab is easy to control, and as long as Jezebel has an Ahab, she will remain. This spirit will not remain where it cannot control.

Leaders who believe they have encountered a Jezebel spirit must ask the Lord for clarity in discerning this spirit. They must themselves walk in total submission to the Lord and those whom He has placed in their lives to lead them. But every leader must purpose in their heart that they will refuse to be an Ahab for a Jezebel.

BREAK THE JEZEBEL SPELL

Jezebel's hold cannot be tolerated over any ministry, and it must be broken. Jesus had some incredibly stern and intense words for the church of Thyatira.

> Nevertheless, I have this against you: You tolerate that woman Jezebel…
> —REVELATION 2:20, NIV

Jesus understood the power and influence of the spirit of Jezebel and wanted this spirit broken off the church in Thyatira. He plainly said that these people tolerated Jezebel. The definition for the English word *tolerate* gives insight into why Jesus made such a statement against this church.

> **Tolerate**—to allow the existence, presence, practice, or act of [something that one does not necessarily like or agree with] without prohibition or hindrance; permit.[1]

What makes this so significant is the fact that not only was the spirit of Jezebel not agreed with, but also she was not interfered with. The leaders of Thyatira allowed her to manifest in their church, and this was tragic! Jezebel will never be conquered unless she is confronted. It was so terrible to Jesus that He said, "I am holding this against you." We must never tolerate what Jesus wants us to obliterate.

Jesus held this tolerant attitude against this church because He was fully cognizant of the damage the spirit of Jezebel could inflict. In the same way He wanted the church in Thyatira to be aware of the spirit of Jezebel, He wants us to be as well. But it is not enough to just be aware of her; she must be dealt with.

FOUR FIGHTING FACTS
(WHY JEZEBEL MUST BE OVERCOME)

1. For the healing of souls

So often when we contend with issues like this, we wind up fighting with people. Jesus never calls us to fight with people; He calls us to fight for them. We must never fight with the person who is being dominated by the spirit of Jezebel. We war with the spirit behind the person. Those who are dominated by Jezebel are tremendously deceived, and they must be delivered lest they be devoured.

Jesus wants to restore those who have fallen and those who are in bondage. In His precious redemptive plan He has made room for everyone. We must reach out in love to those shackled by the enemy, remembering that God is able to deliver them. God loves Jezebels, and so must we. We must love them enough to confront them.

2. For obedience to Christ

When we don't confront Jezebel, God is displeased. We walk in disobedience if we don't rise in the power of the Lord to contend with the spirit of Jezebel. God fully expects us to deny her access to His church. Though it may not be easy to deal with someone controlled by the Jezebel spirit, it will please the Lord when we do it in a right way.

To ignore the spirit of Jezebel is to empower her. Jesus loves His church, and He requires those He has placed in leadership roles to rise during critical times and do things that may make them uncomfortable. Jesus has not empowered us to make us popular; He has empowered us to make us overcomers. We have been fully equipped to overcome the spirit of Jezebel, and we must do so in Jesus's name.

3. For the church to walk in freedom

The Jezebel spirit will hold a church in total and complete chaos and bondage if she is not dealt with. She will destroy its leaders, confuse its attendees, and hinder revival. There is too much at stake to allow her influence to be tolerated over the house and people of God.

I wonder how many churches have not risen to their potential because of the Jezebel spirit. How many pastors have fallen away in discouragement? How many people have been denied a church of power that presents a gospel of hope and freedom? How many are missing heaven? All because, in many ministries, Jezebel sits on the throne instead of Jesus. Jezebel must be dealt with for the church to walk in freedom.

4. For the next generation

Wherever Jezebel is not dealt with, the next generation is at tremendous risk. Revelation 2:23 declares that when Jezebel reigns, the children will not survive. I believe this speaks of a spiritual death.

We must break the power of Jezebel because our children must experience an atmosphere that is bathed in the very presence of God. This generation must see leaders in the church who have pure motives along with no hidden agenda—leaders whose heartbeat is to please the Lord and who possess no desire to glorify self.

Jezebel is self-motivated, self-driven, and self-absorbed. When she is allowed to dominate, our children pay the heaviest price, because they are denied the true expression of the heart of the Father through godly leadership.

How to Break the Jezebel Spell

1. Allow God to deal with you before you deal with anyone else.

This is of extreme importance. When you come against this spirit, it is important that your heart be pure before the Lord. Ask God to guide you, lead you, and direct you. Search your heart and empty yourself of all anger and bitterness toward the person you are confronting.

2. If you are not a spiritual leader, find one.

Recognize your own potential for operating in the Jezebel spirit. It is imperative for you to walk in submission to a God-ordained spiritual leader. You must come to them first and then submit to their council. It is best if they confront the person dominated by this spirit with you.

If this leader says not to approach the person you believe to be under the control of Jezebel, then don't approach them. Realize you have done what you could and should do, and continue to make this a matter of prayer.

3. Approach this person in humility and determination.

Pride is an incredible hindrance to any and all work of the Lord. Be led by the law of love. If you pridefully approach this person, filled with a religious spirit, you have lost before you even started.

This encounter must find its very roots in prayer. Personally submit to the Holy Spirit, and come not only as a revealer but also as a healer. Be determined, but don't be detrimental to this person's life and walk. Your issue is with Jezebel, not the person. Meekness, gentleness, and humility will bring you the victory.

4. Pray, pray, and pray again.

Pray for the person caught by the Jezebel spirit and all Jezebel influences. Prayer binds Jezebel. Declare in faith that every chain of control that this spirit has over the lives of people is destroyed and broken. Declare freedom, healing, joy, and peace in the mighty name of Jesus.

Remember, the power of Christ is greater than the power of Satan, so do not fear! Stand against the stronghold of Jezebel, hold tightly to victory, and do not be denied!

A FIGHT WORTH FIGHTING

It is a tremendous waste of time and energy to fight fights that are not worth fighting. One of the great tragedies in the church is that so often we waste time fighting battles that have no real significance. Satan will come out on top every time if he can keep us focused on things that really don't matter. Carpet colors, musical styles, and grappling over titles and personal agendas are foolish fights. The Jezebel fight, however, is a fight worth fighting.

In the Book of Revelation the church at Thyatira is promised incredible and awesome power to those who pursue through to victory.

> But I also have a message for the rest of you in Thyatira who have not followed this false teaching ("deeper truths," as they call them—depths of Satan, really). I will ask nothing more of you except that you hold tightly to what you have until I come. To all who are victorious, who obey me to the very end, I will give authority over all the nations. They will rule the nations with an iron rod and smash them like clay pots. They will have the same authority I received from my Father, and I will also give them the morning star! Anyone with ears to hear must listen to the Spirit and understand what he is saying to the churches.
> —REVELATION 2:24–29, NLT

These are some amazing promises made here from the very lips of Jesus. Challenging the spirit of Jezebel at the right time, with the right motives, and in the right way will bring incredible benefits to your life and the life of any ministry. Once the spell of Jezebel is broken, the door is open wide for the victory and favor of God to rest on the house. Strife will exit and peace will rush in. New authority and power will arise as the hold of the enemy is broken!

Chapter 7

A SMILING REBELLION

B ETRAYAL ON ANY LEVEL IS ONE OF THE TOUGHEST PILLS OF
all to swallow. It leaves us feeling hurt, vulnerable, and
apprehensive to trust again. It doesn't matter the source; betrayal
hurts. On some level I think most all of us have learned that lesson
somewhere along the line in this journey called life.

Betrayal always stings, doesn't it? But there are different types
and levels of betrayal. It's one thing to be betrayed in business or
by someone who is not heartfelt to us. But betrayal hurts the most
when it occurs at the hands of those we love the most. If you have
ever been betrayed by someone precious to you, you understand
this fact: love is risky business.

No one understood this any better than one of the greatest men
of the Bible who ever lived, King David. His very own son betrayed
him. The story behind this betrayal is one of the most intense in the
entirety of the Word of the Lord. It's a story of sabotage, intrigue,
and disloyalty that resulted in anguish for a father that is impossible to put into words.

BIOGRAPHY OF A BETRAYER

Absalom was born into the ultimate family in all of Israel. He was
the third son of the greatest Jewish king who ever lived. He was
David's pride and joy. His mother's name was Maacah, and his
grandfather was King Talmai of Geshur.

Absalom was born with pedigree and potential. He arrived on the scene in Hebron and moved at an early age to Jerusalem when that amazing city became Israel's capital. Absalom was a favorite of his dad and of the Jewish people as well. He was charismatic and had a great love for protocol and pizzazz. He was the most handsome man in all of Israel.

> In all Israel there was not a man so highly praised for his handsome appearance as Absalom. From the top of his head to the sole of his foot there was no blemish in him.
> —2 SAMUEL 14:25, NIV

Absalom relished the limelight, and if he lived today, he would surely be surrounded by paparazzi and admirers. He lived his life in a grand fashion. He had incredible style and charmed the hearts of the people from the very beginning. He drove a marvelous chariot with fifty men running before him. He was truly an aristocrat in every sense of the word.

Absalom was full of beauty, full of charisma, and, quite sadly, full of himself.

> During his lifetime Absalom had taken a pillar and erected it in the King's Valley as a monument to himself.
> —2 SAMUEL 18:18, NIV

Absalom was filled with pride and absolutely willing to exalt himself.

A MARRED MISSION

Because Absalom never learned and embraced the art of submission, his mission in life was marred. Whenever God gives us a mission, it will always, *always* require submission somewhere in the process.

Absalom had a sister named Tamar whom he was devoted to

and adored. He loved her so much that he named his only daughter after her.

> Whenever God gives us a mission, it will
> always, *always* require submission.

The events surrounding his sister's tragic life were heartbreaking. She was raped by Amnon, her oldest (half) brother, and was devastated by this horrific occurrence. She never got over it, and neither did Absalom.

He spent two bitter years plotting revenge against Amnon and concocted a diabolical scheme. Absalom made a great feast for his brothers in Baalhazor in order to lure his eldest brother into a trap. It was here that Amnon met his vengeful demise, to the joy of Absalom.

It isn't that Amnon certainly did not deserve to be punished for this horrific act against his sister; that is without question. The problem was that it was not Absalom's place to do such a thing or to exact such a price. Whether he agreed with his father, David, or not, it was David's place to deal with the matter and not his. It was this single act of rebellion that first marred what could have been a magnificent mission for the glory of God.

Absalom's actions drove him into exile, and he fled to his grandfather's court in Geshur. He spent three long years there and then made his way back to Jerusalem. It was two more years before he was allowed to see his father again through the intervention of a general in David's army named Joab. For five years the plotter plotted and the schemer schemed. He may have been restored, but he was a restored rebel.

Fueled by offense, hatred, and bitterness, Absalom began to eye his father's throne. This man who had so much was not satisfied with his life. He wanted what was not his at a time when he was not supposed to have it. Absalom used the subtle weapons of kindness, attractiveness, and personality to bring his diabolical agenda into fruition.

WHEN REBELLION SMILES

The Absalom spirit is alive and well in the Christian world today. It is probably the hardest of all to spot. Those who are controlled by the Absalom spirit are like Absalom of the Old Testament. On the surface they are kind, loving, and adored by almost everyone. When a person is surrendered to the spirit of Absalom, he or she looks pious and precious on the outside but is poisoned and polluted on the inside. More often than not these people lead a smiling rebellion against God's ordained leaders.

The true motive of the Absalom spirit is hidden from most people who get tangled in his web of deceit until it is too late. There are many characteristics that you should be aware of when trying to identify whether or not the Absalom spirit has launched an invasion. I want to highlight some of the major ones.

1. Absalom is angry.

Outwardly those controlled by the spirit of Absalom seem calm, cool, and collected. Their composed external demeanor only shields the fiery, volcanic anger that lies just beneath the surface.

Today's version of Absalom is frustrated and irritated with where he or she is in life. He believes he should be more and have more. Inwardly he feels cheated because he is not further along as it relates to his personal ambitions. This frustration only fuels the inferno of anger within that drives him toward rebellion without.

Be careful in aligning yourself with people who seem to be one thing but are actually another. Regardless of how sweetly it is packaged, rebellion is always an outward manifestation of an inward condition. How rebellion manifests is not relevant. What is relevant is this fact: rebellion against God's ordained leader is never acceptable and is always sin.

Absalom of old was angry because he was carrying someone else's offense. He was offended with David because of what had happened to Tamar, and he detested the way in which his father responded. He was absolutely convinced that he would be a better king than David because he would have handled this situation differently.

> Regardless of how sweetly it is packaged,
> rebellion is always an outward
> manifestation of an inward condition.

The bottom line was that Absalom was mad, and Absalom wanted his way. Those controlled by the spirit of Absalom are mad, and they want their way. Not only do they want their way, but they will also do anything to get it!

It is very interesting to me that Absalom's mother's name was Maacah. I find this intriguing because of the original meaning of her name. The name *Maacah* means oppression. So in a literal sense Absalom was the child of oppression. Oppression is a terrible thing. The word oppression has as its root the word *oppress*. Webster's dictionary defines the word *oppress* like this.

> **Oppress**—to crush or burden by abuse of power or authority[1]

Absalom, this son of oppression, was mad because he perceived he was being oppressed by David unjustly. In his mind David stood in his way. His perception was that David oppressed, blocked, and hindered him from becoming who he thought he should be.

The feeling of oppression, whether perceived or legitimate, is challenging to say the least. When someone is controlled by the spirit of Absalom, they feel oppressed and justified in their anger and response to their leader. Just as Absalom justified his rebellion, people in the church do as well.

Someone controlled by the spirit of Absalom can easily legitimize their treasonous acts of rebellion, however in error they may be. They believe they are being oppressed and limited by their leader. The spirit of Absalom is not restricted to the church only; very often it will manifest itself in the workplace.

Disaster is on the horizon when we position ourselves in league with those who are offended and angry at God's ordained authority. But as we study the story of Absalom, sadly we find that many in Israel were deceived and did just that.

2. Absalom becomes a judge in an effort to become a king.

Absalom was convinced it was his right to judge everyone and everything. The first example of this is found when he acted as judge and jury with his brother Amnon and had him killed. You may be thinking, "Absalom is not so bad; he meant well and was sincere." Quite honestly, Absalom may have been sincere, but he was sincerely wrong. Sincerity does not change what is wrong and what is right. It was not the place of Absalom to have Amnon killed, nor was it his place to judge David. Judging is very addictive. Just say no!

Becoming judge was the first step that led Absalom down the path of destruction. He became a judge in an effort to become king. Those who have the Absalom spirit will judge everything and everyone who is in authority. This is necessary for them to be able to gain power and influence.

Absalom masterminded this process brilliantly. Even though he was not called or qualified, he began to package himself as Israel's next king.

> In the course of time, Absalom provided himself with a
> chariot and horses and with fifty men to run ahead of

him. He would get up early and stand by the side of the road leading to the city gate. Whenever anyone came with a complaint to be placed before the king for a decision, Absalom would call out to him, "What town are you from?" He would answer, "Your servant is from one of the tribes of Israel." Then Absalom would say to him, "Look, your claims are valid and proper, but there is no representative of the king to hear you." And Absalom would add, "If only I were appointed judge in the land! Then everyone who has a complaint or case could come to me and I would see that they receive justice."

—2 SAMUEL 15:1–4, NIV

Absalom was a brilliant tactician and was very pragmatic in his approach. He presented himself to be more than he was. It was all very grand. He provided himself with chariots and horses and fifty men to run before him. He was an amazing promoter of all things Absalom. When people saw him, they could not help but be impressed. Absalom brilliantly manipulated every situation to his advantage.

Even when he began to undermine David, he was incredibly sly in the process. He judged David, though he never even called his name. He just said, "If I were in charge around here, things would be different." He told these gullible people, "Folks like you would matter to me," implying that they did not matter to David. He had to become a critical judge of David if he had any hope of deceiving the people.

3. Absalom competes for an audience.

Absalom viewed David not as his leader but as his competitor. David possessed the position that he desired to have. When someone is ruled by the spirit of Absalom, whether in the church world or the cooperate world, he sees leadership as competition. In discrediting leadership, Absalom empowers his own ego-driven, self-advancing agenda.

Absalom understood that in order to rule the people, he would have to win the people. He would rise early in the morning and go to the gates of the city and intercept the people because he had a handle on the amazing the power of influence. Whoever has the power to influence you, in a very real way, has won you. Absalom was trying to win the people because ultimately he wanted to win the crown.

It is the same with the Absalom-driven person today; he seeks to win an audience because he is in competition with his leader. To those with the Absalom spirit, people are not to be loved and led but rather a commodity to be spent in order to buy their desired position. Absalom leaders use people to gain position and power. True leaders use their position to empower and bless people. In the eyes of heaven people are priceless. God is most concerned not about position or title but about His people.

> The LORD's portion is His people.
> —DEUTERONOMY 32:9

The word *portion* is translated from the powerful Hebrew word *cheleq*, which means "chosen part" or "great priority." Heaven's greatest priority is the people for whom Christ died. People are not to be recruited to join sides in a war for position. When this occurs, Absalom is on the loose.

It is a shameful thing for a spirit of competition to rest in the church. There is unbridled joy in Satan's kingdom when this takes place. He knows that as long as we are competing with each other, we are ignoring him.

When leaders have victories and breakthroughs, Absalom cannot rejoice for the win. He will silently seethe, strategizing on how he can lessen the impact of the victory and galvanize the people's hearts away from the leader and toward himself. Why? Because without an audience Absalom is powerless.

4. Absalom operates through division and diversion because he seeks to devour.

Absalom sought to divide the people and to alienate them from David. He accomplished this through undermining David's leadership. Absalom knew that the key to devouring the people was dividing them. He diverted the attention of the people off of David and onto himself.

When you break the word *division* down, it really explains the powerful tactics that Absalom employed. There are two parts to this word, *di* and *vision*. *Di* actually comes from the Greek language and was originally *dis*. *Dis* means "two, or more than one." *Di* and *vision* are more than one vision. So when Absalom rises up, he wants to impart a different vision. The vision he wants to deposit in people's lives is his own vision.

Absalom, this masterful manipulator, did everything he could do to divert the people away from their leader, David. He constantly found fault with David, and he did so not through major things but through small things. He was consistently negative about everything. He used half truths, facial expressions, and innuendos to cause people to lose faith and confidence in David.

> Giftedness does not qualify the leader; God does.

This is exactly what the Absalom spirit does. He rises up, questioning and critical. Comments are carefully carved arrows of destruction that are aimed straight for the heart. Absalom always seeks to turn the hearts of the people away from their leader. At its very core the Absalom spirit is a ravenous devourer who only seeks to satisfy his appetite for power.

5. Absalom leads a smiling rebellion.

Love, kindness, and compliments are his weapons of choice. What's wrong with that, and who can resist him? He smiles as he festers and facilitates rebellion. He works very hard to make his victims feel special. He acts concerned and caring, but in reality he is only positioning himself for his ultimate goal: *takeover.* His tactics are deliberate and deadly.

> Also, whenever anyone approached him to bow down before him, Absalom would reach out his hand, take hold of him and kiss him. Absalom behaved in this way toward all the Israelites who came to the king asking for justice, and so he stole the hearts of the men of Israel.
>
> —2 SAMUEL 15:5–6, NIV

Absalom stole the hearts of the people through fake concern. He was beautiful, gifted, and articulate, *but he wasn't called to lead.* Everyone loved Absalom, even David. But Absalom was evil. Giftedness does not qualify the leader; God does.

Absalom led a smiling rebellion as he seduced the hearts of the people. Sadly, smiling rebellions are still being led today.

AN ABSALOM ENCOUNTER

You may have encountered the spirit of Absalom in the past and not even known it. If you haven't, get ready; you more than likely will. An encounter with someone controlled by the spirit of Absalom unfolds something like this.

Absalom may begin by praising himself. He will tell you all that he is doing, the people he is connected to, and the great favor over his life. Remember, Absalom of old sought to impress the people of Israel. Those controlled by the spirit of Absalom today do exactly that; they seek to impress.

At some point this person will compliment and encourage you. He will do everything possible to make you feel great about yourself. He will tell you how special you are and how much you matter. In the natural you will probably enjoy this and even appreciate it.

This modern-day Absalom will act incredibly concerned about

you or those precious to you. All this seems so heartfelt. What could be wrong with any of this? This individual is so loving and so caring. He smiles the smile of concern, but just remember: he is leading a smiling rebellion.

The conversation will shift at some point. He (or she) will begin to bait you with questions, trying to determine your position on issues within the church or company. He will talk about the pastor and leadership and declare he is only concerned. Nothing they do satisfies him.

He sows seeds of doubt. He can't really identify major things, so he jumps on minor things. He questions things such as the expensiveness of the pastor's car, why he takes so many offerings, why he does this, or how come he doesn't do that. He never comes out and says it, but you know he is seeking a change in leadership. You become aware of the fact that he is nominating himself to become leader! He is doing everything he can to bring you into his camp.

This Absalom may smile, but he is hell inspired. He believes himself to be a legitimate leader and wants you to see it as well. He will tell you what you want to hear in order to gain your allegiance. A true pastor and leader will not tell you what you want to hear; he or she will tell you what you need to hear. Absalom attempts to awaken an offense within you against your leader; he surrounds himself with offended people.

You must identify this spirit at work and have nothing to do with it! The spirit of Absalom is to the soul what a malignant tumor is to the body: it is deadly.

ABSALOM WAS THE ARCHITECT
OF HIS OWN DEMISE

Absalom's motives became clear when he stole the kingdom from David, but his rebellion was doomed to failure. He hijacked his father's throne for a season. He was so depraved that he slept with David's wives and claimed them as his own. His hatred for David was obvious and exposed at this point. Never forget; Absalom is depraved, and you must not become a part of that depravity. Avoid Absalom at all costs.

Judgment fell on Absalom, and not only did he lose the position and the throne, but he also lost his life. He experienced the "ultimate bad hair day." Absalom got caught on the limb of an oak tree by his beautiful hair while he was riding a donkey. David's men saw him and told General Joab. Joab killed Absalom on the spot by running three spears through his heart.

In the spiritual sense the only hope for the Absaloms of today is death to their wicked heart. God can give them a new heart, but the old rebellious and sinful heart must die.

> I will give you a new heart and put a new spirit in you;
> I will remove from you your heart of stone and give you
> a heart of flesh.
> —EZEKIEL 36:26, NIV

God is able to change an Absalom heart, but Absalom must be willing.

The saddest part of Absalom's story is the fact that he could have very well become king. His younger brother, Solomon, actually ascended to the throne, but Absalom was in line ahead of him. There is no telling how greatly God would have used him if he would have been able to control himself. He didn't have to die an untimely and unfortunate death, but he was the architect of his own demise.

However, Absalom doesn't bear all the blame. David failed Absalom. David failed him because he never dealt with him. He loved him too much to do so, and it cost them both. Whether in the church or the workplace, Absalom must be confronted in love by a leader. Absalom cannot be allowed to bring division through alienating and deceiving people within the church or company.

How to Contend With the Absalom Spirit

1. Ask God for clarity.

Pray and ask the Lord to show you whatever you need to see. Look for the signs and characteristics of Absalom in the life of the person you are concerned about.

2. Seek counsel from your legitimate spiritual leader.

Do not confront Absalom alone and without the permission from the leader of the church or business. Submit to the council of whoever is in charge, and then pray fervently for the Lord to cause His will to be done in this situation.

3. Do all things in love.

You will never go wrong if you allow love to lead you. Even if the person controlled by the spirit of Absalom has to leave or causes trouble, avoid taking up an offense. Everything you do concerning this matter must be done in the love of Jesus

4. Allow God to contend with the person controlled by the Absalom spirit.

God dealt with the Absalom of the Old Testament, and He will deal with the Absaloms and their followers of today. Absalom will destroy himself.

God will do what needs to be done, and we must trust Him. There may even be a season where it seems like Absalom has won, but wait on the Lord; He will contend with Absalom. Do what you are able, and then turn it over to Jesus.

5. Never be a part of a smiling rebellion.

Anyway you slice it, rebellion is wrong. Determine in your heart never to allow yourself to be caught in the trap of Absalom. No matter how good he makes it look.

Reject a divisive man [or woman] after the first and second admonition, knowing that such a person is warped and sinning, being self-condemned.

—Titus 3:10–11

Place your allegiance firmly behind God's ordained leader. Do not entertain negative or slanderous talk about them. When you do so, rejoice! You have broken the power of the Absalom spirit over your life. You are prepared for God's best as you follow God's true leader into your future!

Chapter 8

The RUNAWAY BRIDE

I
T WAS A BEAUTIFUL FALL EVENING IN 1988 IN TAMPA, FLORIDA, and love was in the air. A nervous and excited young man stood on the stage of a small church, watching the girl of his dreams as she came walking down the aisle. This dark-haired, hazel-eyed beauty had stolen his heart. Her stunning white gown glistened in the candlelight as she came toward him in what seemed like slow motion. She had bought this dress at a reasonable price and spent days painstakingly sewing hundreds of sequins on it, one at a time.

Every eye in the place was resting on her, but none more fervently and intensely than his. Even though every seat was full, to him, in that magical moment, only she was in the room. This was the one, the one he had hoped for, the one he had prayed for, and here she was, and there could never be another.

His heart almost skipped a beat when the pastor asked, "Who gives this woman to be married to this man?"

Her dad replied, "Her mother and I."

He took her by the hand twenty-four years ago, and he has been holding it ever since.

There wasn't a lot of money available for an extravagant rehearsal dinner or a magnificent wedding reception. There was some cake and punch. This young couple didn't have much in the way of material things, but they were rich where it counted. They were rich in love.

That love-struck young man was me, and that gorgeous bride

was my wife, Dawn, and I am truly blessed. Three kids, twenty-four years, and a boatload of adventures later, we are still going strong. To quote those incredible philosophers and theologians, the Isley Brothers, "Love Is a Wonderful Thing."

I can't even imagine what it would have been like if Dawn would have left me standing at the altar. If she would have been a runaway bride that night, she would have shattered my love-filled heart into a million pieces. Putting all bravado aside, when you love someone like that, that person has incredible power over your life.

Isn't it amazing that as believers and followers of Jesus we are called the bride of Christ? The love Jesus has for you is immense and immeasurable. It was a love so great that it carried Him to the cross and beyond.

THE BRIDE OF CHRIST

The process of Jewish courtship and marriage is one of the most beautiful expressions of the love of Jesus. An understanding of this process brings real clarity to why we as the church are called the bride of Christ. Let me quickly describe these beautiful steps with you.

1. The marriage is arranged and the bride is selected.

It's amazing to be chosen. It was no small thing for a Jewish bride to be selected. The groom's mother and father would choose the best bride they could for their son. And there is something very powerful that you must understand: no matter how you feel about yourself—no matter your past, no matter your issues, no matter your self-doubt, no matter what—you have been chosen. God chose you.

> Ye have not chosen me, but I have chosen you.
> —JOHN 15:16, KJV

> But ye are a chosen generation.
> —1 PETER 2:9, KJV

God did it, Jesus declares it, and Peter reinforces it, but it's not relevant until you believe it. On your best day or your worst, one thing does not change: you are chosen by the Lord. You must grasp this in no uncertain terms: you are chosen. Failures, frictions, fractions, and all: you, my friend, are chosen.

2. A dowry is paid for the bride.

Throughout the Bible we see examples of this. Remember the story of Jacob, who worked seven years for the hand of Rachel and wound up having to work seven more because Laban deceived him. What would drive a man to work for fourteen years in order to gain a woman's hand in marriage? One thing: love!

> Jacob was in love with Rachel and said, "I'll work for you seven years in return for your younger daughter Rachel." Laban said, "It's better that I give her to you than to some other man. Stay here with me." So Jacob served seven years to get Rachel, but they seemed like only a few days to him because of his love for her.
> —GENESIS 29:18–20, NIV

Jacob was madly in love with Rachel, and he was willing to pay the price, no matter how steep. Love had captured him and would hold him in place, no matter what.

As the bride of Christ each of us must realize that the dowry offered by the Father was extravagant and extreme.

> For you were bought at a price.
> —1 CORINTHIANS 6:20

> Knowing that you were not redeemed with corruptible things, like silver or gold, from your aimless conduct received by tradition from your fathers, but with the precious blood of Christ, as of a lamb without blemish and without spot.
> —1 PETER 1:18–19

Jesus paid the price for all He has redeemed. It was a price that in the natural was so great that as He prayed in the garden, He desired to relent. But He did not. He knew that the bride price had to be paid, and only He could pay it.

Many think that as He hung on the cross—marred, mangled and mutilated—the nails were what held Him in His place. Some think it might have been the brutality and threat of the Roman soldiers that held Him there. But you know what? It was not the nails or the guards or anything else of man's doing. What held Him in His place was one thing: love.

Jesus paid the bride price for you because He loved you. He believed you were worth it. Even when you don't, He always did and He always will.

Hebrews 12:24 says that the blood of Jesus spoke as He shed it for you and me two thousand years ago. Every drop of blood that spilled from His wounded and trembling body declared volumes to each one of us who are now His bride. Every drop said three words: "I love you."

There's not a love song or love story that has ever been written that even comes close to that. The romance of redemption is the greatest romance of all.

3. A mutual choosing takes place.

When Rebekah was chosen to marry Isaac, Abraham wanted to be sure that the feelings were reciprocal.

> "If the woman is not willing to follow you, then you will be released from this oath of mine."...So they called Rebekah and asked her, "Will you go with this man?" "I will go," she said.
> —GENESIS 24:8, 58, NIV

It wasn't enough that Rebekah was chosen; she was required to make a choice herself. She had to choose to marry Isaac. What is powerful about this story is that Abraham actually sent his servant

Eliezer to Rebekah to tell her she had been selected. She decided to marry Isaac though she had never seen him

It is the same for us as Christians; as the bride of Christ we have never seen Him. And in the same way that Abraham sent Eliezer, the heavenly Father has sent the Holy Spirit to us to inform us that we have been chosen. But it is our responsibility to choose the Lord right back. Many years ago I chose my wife, but our marriage would have never occurred if she had not chosen me right back.

The Bible says that we are made in the image and likeness of God. By His very nature God is sovereign. That means He is in charge; He has the ability to choose. It seems natural, then, that if we are made in the image of God, a sovereign God would create a sovereign man.

This does not mean that we are all gods; it means that we are sovereign over our lives. We make our own decisions and choices concerning ourselves.

> This day I call heaven and earth as witnesses against you that I have set before you life and death, blessings and curses. Now choose life, so that you and your children may live.
> —DEUTERONOMY 30:19, NIV

> Choose for yourselves this day whom you will serve.
> —JOSHUA 24:15

You have a choice. You have been chosen, but you must choose the Lord right back. There are some who believe that God chooses some and rejects others.

I personally cannot believe that when children, whom God created, are born, some are born chosen and some are born rejected. My firm conviction is this: God has chosen every human being that has and will ever be born. He has chosen you, your children, and their children. He is a God of love, and He has chosen us all.

> For God so loved the world, that he gave his only
> begotten son.
>
> —JOHN 3:16, KJV

God so loves the whole world that He gave His one and only Son, Jesus, as sin's offering for us all.

> In the same way your Father in heaven is not willing
> that any of these little ones should be lost.
>
> —MATTHEW 18:14, NIV

> The Lord is not slack concerning His promise, as some
> count slackness, but is longsuffering toward us, not
> willing that any should perish but that all should come
> to repentance.
>
> —2 PETER 3:9

God is not willing for or wanting anyone to perish; He has chosen everyone. But sadly everyone will not choose Him back.

The choice must be made continually. Every day I choose to be married to my wife, and she chooses to be married to me. We chose to remain faithful to each other and to honor our vows of marriage. I pray we always will. But we must continually choose.

I am so thankful that not only has Jesus chosen us, but also we have chosen Him right back. Purpose in your heart to chose Him afresh every day!

4. The groom provides a written covenant.

This covenant the groom provided was a written document stating the bride price that would be paid. It also contained the promises of the groom and the rights of the bride. The groom obligated himself to fulfill every promise contained in the covenant agreement of marriage.

It is a wonderful thing as the bride of Christ to recognize and realize that Jesus has provided a written covenant containing our rights and promises. As the bride of Christ our legal document is the New Testament.

> For no matter how many promises God has made, they are "Yes" in Christ. And so through him the "Amen" is spoken by us to the glory of God.
> —2 CORINTHIANS 1:20, NIV

As the bride of Christ you have the right to claim every single promise that is recorded in the Word of God. It's in your covenant! The bride price purchased healing, deliverance, joy, peace, financial provision, and more.

When you face situations that you cannot handle, pull out your written covenant, the Bible. Lay claim to every promise that is rightfully yours according to the Word of the Lord. Whatever it says you have, you have. You don't have to negotiate to get it, nor do you have to earn it. As the bride of Jesus it is yours!

In faith remind your need of your covenant. Believe and receive every promise God has made you. Agree with what the covenant says. When you read a scripture on healing, provision, or anything else you're trusting for, read it in faith. Joyfully apply it to your circumstance and declare, "Yes and amen!"

5. *The bridal pledge gift is given.*

Once the bride accepted the groom's proposal, the groom would provide a gift to the bride as a pledge. When he gave his bride this gift, it was his way of promising his bride that he would fulfill his promise of marriage. It was to give the bride assurance that he was serious and could be relied on.

The practice of giving this gift is like our giving an engagement ring today. It says, "I am getting married." Every girl who gets engaged loves to show off her ring. She doesn't hide the ring or refuse to wear it. On the contrary, she walks around and shows it off! She wants her ring to shine.

As the bride of Christ we should be happily aware of the fact that Jesus has provided us with the greatest gift imaginable. He has given us the gift of the Holy Spirit.

Paul called the gift of the Holy Spirit the "earnest…in our hearts" (1 Cor. 1:22, KJV). When you are going to purchase something important like a house or a car, you are often expected to put earnest money down. This money shows that you are serious and intend on following through with the purchase. The Holy Spirit is our guarantee!

> Who hath also sealed us, and given the earnest of the Spirit in our hearts.
> —2 CORINTHIANS 1:22, KJV

Jesus gave us the Holy Spirit as an earnest gift. He was declaring this was our earnest or down payment. The Holy Spirit is our engagement ring!

As believers we are adorned with a living engagement ring: *the Holy Spirit of God!* We should not shamefully hide Him away, but we should allow the power of the Holy Spirit to shine brightly in our lives.

The Holy Spirit is the gift that keeps on giving. The Holy Spirit gives power, boldness, clarity—not to mention the nine gifts of the Spirit that are accessible for us as the bride of Christ. The Holy Spirit is a huge gift from Jesus. If we were to compare the Holy Spirit to an engagement ring, He would be the ultimate bling!

6. The espousal (engagement) period takes place.

At this point it's officially official! The bride and groom are espoused, engaged, and betrothed. We (the church) are at this moment espoused to Christ. We are engaged to Jesus.

Our bridegroom has paid the most incredible bride price ever. He has laid His own life down and provided a dowry that will remain unmatched through the ages. He has also given us the Holy Spirit as our betrothal gift. But this is not the end; on the contrary, this is only the beginning.

In Jewish tradition the groom was expected to go and be with his father for a season. It was his duty to build his bride a home or an addition onto the house. Before he left the bride, he would make this statement: "I go to prepare a place for you, and if I am going, I will return again to you." Sound familiar? If it doesn't, it should. These are the very words that came from the lips of Jesus relating to His bride.

> In My Father's house are many mansions: if it were not so, I would have told you. I go to prepare a place for you. And if I go and prepare a place for you, I will come again and receive you to Myself.
> —JOHN 14:2–3

Jesus has pledged to us that He will come again. He has prepared a place for us, and where He is, we will go. Isn't that just awesome? We have assurance that Jesus will come again. Let me reinforce that fact: Jesus is coming again! I believe it because He said He was.

I heard a little story one time about a young man who said, "Jesus said it, I believe it, and that settles it!" An old grandmother looked at this young man and smiled as she replied, "Jesus said it, and that settles it whether you believe it or not!"

This story has incredible meaning to us today because many no longer hold to the belief that Jesus is coming again to receive His bride in the Rapture. But it is settled; He is coming. The fact that some don't believe it changes nothing; our Bridegroom shall return!

Now there is something very important to note. Biblical engagement is considered as fully binding as marriage, so much so that unfaithfulness on the part of the bride-to-be or groom-to-be is considered adultery. The couple is expected to live virtuously during the time of engagement. No side relationships or flirting around are allowed during this period. As Christians we must remember that we are espoused to our loving Bridegroom, Jesus. He loves us with a radical, real, and everlasting love. It is our duty to remain faithful to Him. He has proven His great love to us. He has loved us when in times past we were altogether unlovely. He deserves our committed heartfelt affection. We should remain true to Him as our ultimate love. We should not allow ourselves to be seduced by lesser lovers. Anyone, anything, or any activity is so much less when compared to Jesus.

We need to wear His engagement ring, the Holy Spirit. The Holy Spirit present in our life will remind us to be faithful to Him. That precious gift from Jesus will cause us to remember His goodness and grace in times of temptation.

As His bride we are to remain consecrated and set apart. We keep ourselves ready for the return of our Bridegroom. In ancient times when the bride left her house, she would wear a veil. The veil symbolized to everyone that she was taken. In like manner, as believers and brides of Christ, we also wear a spiritual veil that covers us.

> Therefore, brethren, having boldness to enter the Holiest
> by the blood of Jesus, by a new and living way which He
> consecrated for us, through the veil, that is, His flesh.
> —HEBREWS 10:19–20

Being consecrated through the veil of the flesh of Jesus is like being covered with His blood. Our lives are viewed through that veil. Our stained past is taken care of and even viewed through the veil of the precious blood of Jesus. The Bible tells us in Revelation 7:14 that we are washed and made clean through the blood of Jesus.

We now await the coming of our Bridegroom, Jesus. As we wait, we are covered by His precious blood. It is our veil, and we wear it as we await his return.

The love of Jesus is incomparable and incomprehensible. He has chosen us to be His bride, and what holds our relationship together is love. Every sound relationship must have as its foundation one central thing: love. A relationship built on anything less than that is doomed for disaster.

THE RUNAWAY BRIDE

Some of the most sobering words written in the Bible were spoken by Jesus and recorded by John the Revelator on the island of Patmos. These telling words are directed to the church of Ephesus.

> To the angel of the church of Ephesus write, "These things says He who holds the seven stars in His right hand, who walks in the midst of the seven golden lamp-stands: 'I know your works, your labor, your patience, and that you cannot bear those who are evil. And you have tested those who say they are apostles and are not, and have found them liars; and you have persevered and have patience, and have labored for My name's sake and have not become weary. Nevertheless I have this against you, that you have left your first love. Remember there-fore from where you have fallen; repent and do the first works, or else I will come to you quickly and remove your lampstand from its place—unless you repent. But this you have, that you hate the deeds of the Nicolaitans, which I also hate. He who has an ear, let him hear what the Spirit says to the churches. To him who overcomes I will give to eat from the tree of life, which is in the midst of the Paradise of God.'"
>
> —REVELATION 2:1–7

I am convinced these words must have been heartbreaking for John to hear and record. John comprehended love in a way that none of the other disciples grasped.

John is the one who penned the words in John 3:16, "For God so loved the world." He also spoke much of love in his epistle of 1 John. He spoke of the "love the Father has bestowed on us, that we should be called children of God" (1 John 3:1). He went on to exhort the church by admonishing us to "love one another" (v. 11). In 1 John 4:7 he said that "love is of God; and everyone who loves is born of God and knows God." He even said in verse 8, "He who does not love does not know God."

In the New Testament one out of every three verses on the subject of love was written by John. Church tradition says that as an old man living in Ephesus, his disciples would carry him into the services on a cot. Many expected him to speak of the times he walked with Jesus and saw firsthand His miraculous power and resurrection. But tradition says he would lift up his tired old head and begin to weakly whisper to the church. Every ear would strain to hear what this old apostle was saying. Over and over again he whispered these words, "Little children, love each other."

Can you imagine as John stood on Patmos and heard the words of Jesus? How it must have affected him! The church he loved was turning into a loveless church. The church was in grave danger of becoming a runaway bride.

Jesus even begins His conversation concerning the church in Ephesus with acknowledging good things about them. Jesus said several things that must be noted and not neglected.

1. Labor can never replace love.

Jesus told them He knew their works and their labors. *Works* refers to activities. If the church in Ephesus were in your town today, it would be a church filled with activities. It would have a place for every age group, and everyone could be involved.

Jesus said He knew their labors. The word *labor* means toil and effort put into labor. Ephesus was a church that labored hard. Every impacting church has to have those who work hard in order for it to be successful.

Listen to the kind of language Jesus uses to describe this church in Ephesus.

- He said that they had borne. The word *borne* means to bear what is burdensome.

- He commended them for having patience. *Patience* in this scripture means steadfastness and endurance.

- Jesus goes on to say to them that they had "not fainted" (Rev. 2:3, KJV). That means that even though they were intensely persecuted and relentlessly attacked because of their belief in Jesus, they did not quit or grow weary.

They did all this work for the Lord, but they were falling out of love with the Lord of the work. It happens so much even today. People fall in love with the activity of the ministry and lose sight of what drew them into ministry in the first place: simply Jesus.

2. Doctrine alone will never replace devotion.

They were a church that held to sound doctrine. They could have told you what they believed and why they believed it.

> And you have tested those who say they are apostles and are not, and have found them liars.
> —REVELATION 2:2

They tested those who said they were representatives and apostles of Christ but were not. False doctrine was not allowed in their church; they wouldn't have it! They would only allow truth to be taught in their church.

Doctrine devoid of devotion leads to death. They had lists without love and rules without relationship. My, how we need sound doctrine these days, but make no mistake about it: doctrine will never replace devotion.

At first glance, who would not desire to be a part of this working, active, doctrinally sound church? They seemed so in love with the ministry and in doing the right thing. But a closer look revealed a church filled with a loveless bride.

A loveless bride will soon become a runaway bride. This loveless church was spellbound by their rituals and their rules. They knew church business well, but they could not continue to operate effectively without the fuel of love.

What brought the church in Ephesus to the point of being a runaway bride? How did they go from a church all about love to a church that was all out of love? I think the answers might be easier to discover than you think. Just look at what creates a runaway bride in the natural sense.

Fear of total commitment

Fear can certainly overtake a runaway bride. Committing to marriage in the natural sense is a very intense thing. Marriage is a total commitment. It is saying to one another, "I am here for you for the rest of my life, and you can count on that."

Many Christians turn into runaway brides of Christ because they have a fear of total commitment to Jesus. They are unwilling to honestly declare, "Lord, I am totally committed to You and will remain so the rest of my life." There is so little total commitment today to anything. But following Jesus and becoming His bride requires total and true commitment.

Lack of trust

Any marriage that is empty of trust will be a hollow one. If either party feels like they can't trust the other, the marriage relationship is in trouble.

It's one thing to say you love Jesus, but part of really loving Him is learning how to trust Him. Even when we go through situations we don't understand, we must trust Him.

Trust puts love to the test. There are seasons and times when love will require us to trust the Lord when we cannot track Him. We are called to trust in the Lord with all our heart and to lean not to our own understanding. (See Proverbs 3:5.) Our own understanding is just that. It's our own understanding—it's limited, its finite, it's flawed. This is why we must trust the Lord, because He has knowledge that is eternal and perfect.

In marriage we must be able to trust our mates with all our hearts. As believers we must trust the Lord with all our hearts as well.

Many times the reason a bride runs away is because she is sabotaged by a lack of trust. Often those who start out following Jesus don't finish their journey because when times get hard, they fail to trust. But I would say to you even as you read this book, trust Jesus. I am living proof that at times we all face seasons that are challenging, to say the least. But trust Him. It pays to trust Jesus. The Bible says in Romans 8:28, "All things work together for good to those who love God."

The Lord is concerned about two things—your good and His glory—so trust Him.

Lack of intimacy

Intimate times spent together are the key to making any relationship work. So often we place intimacy into a single category and make it sexual. But intimacy is so much more than a sexual experience.

Intimacy in a relationship is the process of becoming familiar with someone. This occurs through investing time, effort, and energy into the relationship. You can't love someone you know nothing about. To be intimate with someone means that we have developed a personal heartfelt tie with him or her. Lasting relationships are intimate ones.

In Ephesus the people had relationship with one another and with church activity itself. This is good. Church should be a place where you develop strong relationships with other believers, as well as a place to serve. But the main goal of the church, however, is to develop an atmosphere where people are drawn into a deeper relationship with Jesus.

Servanthood and relationships within the church itself should be an outflow of our relationship with Jesus. Relationship with Jesus is the key and catalyst for everything else.

The very first step to becoming a runaway bride is when we live lives of prayerlessness.

The path to intimacy with Jesus is found through spending time in His Word, in worship, and in prayer. Intimacy requires investment. Anytime there is not a sufficient amount of time invested in intimacy, any relationship will suffer. And this is true even as it relates to Christ; we must invest in Him if we are to know Him.

Many people think that a person becomes a spiritual runaway bride when he or she leaves the church. This is not true. We are in greatest danger of becoming a runaway bride when we leave the altar. Jesus can always be encountered at the altar of prayer, but many times we leave Him standing at the altar. The greatest intimacy with the Lord is realized at the altar of prayer. The very first step to becoming a runaway bride is when we live lives of prayerlessness. Prayerlessness leads to carelessness.

We must never think we can replace the altar of intimacy with religious activity. This very moment your Bridegroom, Jesus, is waiting at the altar for an encounter with you. Have you left Him at the altar?

Past baggage

One of the greatest obstacles many couples contend with in their relationships is overcoming the baggage of their past. We can find it hard to love what *is* if we allow ourselves to be held captive by what *was*. It can be difficult to forgive yourself (or someone you're in relationship with) when you haven't gotten over the past. As long the past is not released, it will be baggage.

Satan loves for us to carry the baggage of our past into our relationship with Jesus. He is fully aware that as long as we carry the baggage of our past failures and sins, we are hindered in developing a truly intimate relationship with Jesus.

Baggage is bondage.

As believers it is important to know that Jesus never holds our past against us, ever. It's not that He doesn't know what we have done or He doesn't recall it. But He chooses not to remember it and hold it against us. Wow! That is powerful. Our baggage is never His. No matter how total and complete our failures in life have been, Jesus never fails in forgiveness. In fact, the Bible gives us great assurance in the Book of Psalms concerning this reality.

> He has removed our sins as far from us as the east is
> from the west.
> —PSALM 103:12, NLT

Satan will do everything he can to remind us of our past issues and failures. He is masterful at convincing us that we could never truly be forgiven, that the stains of our past are too great. He wants us to be so weighted down that we could never enter into a true and loving relationship with Jesus.

But Jesus died so we could get past our past.

Satan will try to convince us that it is pointless to pray or even worship. He wants us to believe that we are totally unworthy because of our past or that our worship is not desired or received by the Lord. But he is a liar.

We don't worship the Lord because *we're* worthy; we worship the Lord because *He* is. Let the baggage of the past go; Jesus has.

Other lovers

Now, this is a biggie! It's not possible to develop a viable relationship with someone if you have your eyes on other lovers. Many a bride has run from the altar where her groom waited and ran into the arms of another man. That would be an incredibly heart-wrenching event for anyone, bride or groom.

Anytime a runaway bride abandons her groom for someone

else, this didn't happen overnight. Her seduction may have been mindful and methodical, but never forget: she was willing.

When he whispered, she listened. When she watched him, she longed. When he won her, she lost. She listened. She longed. She lost.

There will always be other loves that seek to steal our gaze away from Jesus. Have you ever had other loves vie for your attention? People or things that want to pull you from the arms of Jesus? It can be money, success, wrong relationships, prideful religion, and even church work. But there is no other love that compares to the love of Christ.

Love Will Keep Us Together!

When I was a kid the Captain and Tennille had a hit song titled "Love Will Keep Us Together." My sister had the record, and she and I listened to that song so much that we knew every word! I could sing it all even now. (I have so much useless information in my mind!)

The words of that song are appropriate in a way to our relationship with Jesus: love *will* keep us together. Jesus said to the church in Ephesus, "I have this against you, that you have left your first love" (Rev. 2:4). Jesus takes love very seriously. He wants more than "motion"; He wants "emotion." Emotion for Jesus should be what puts us in motion for Him.

The church in Ephesus was spellbound by their own religion and activity. Jesus gave them a powerful remedy that, if followed, would bring His bride back around.

> Remember therefore from where you have fallen; repent and do the first works.
> —Revelation 2:5

Jesus told them first to remember. The word *remember* is translated from the Greek word *mnemoneuo*. This word involves more than just recalling something. It means to think of a person or a thing and to feel emotion while you do.

So Jesus wanted them to remember a couple of things. He wanted them to call to mind what they used to be. He desired for them to recall the bondage and idolatry of their past. He had brought them so far and set them free from so much. He knew if they could remember what they used to be, it would reawaken their love for Him.

It is the same with us. We have all had times in our lives when our love for Jesus was not at the level it should have been. In those moments we should hit the rewind button of life. We should remember and recall how very far the Lord has brought us and how His great love has transformed our lives. The very fact that He loved us when we were yet in our sins should awaken anew a passionate love for Jesus.

There was another reason Christ wanted them to remember the height from where they had fallen. At one time they had obviously had a rich and real relationship with Him. The longer they served Jesus, they began to try to replace labor with love. So Jesus wanted them to return to the time when they did the things they did out of a deep and abiding love, not out of religious duty. He wanted to awaken in them a longing for His presence once again.

Have you ever longed for Jesus? I know I have. Our lives are lived at their apex when we live them close to Jesus. We are kinder, more loving, more patient, and more powerful when we are in right relationship with the Lord. Quite honestly the happiest times I have ever had are those when I have felt closest to Jesus.

Do you feel distant from Jesus? Why not stop right now and remember? Remember how beautiful your closest times have been with the Lord, and seek that place again.

The next thing Jesus told the church in Ephesus to do was to repent. *Repent* is translated from the Greek word *metanoeo*. It is an incredible word that means more than just saying I am sorry. So often we see repentance in the church as just a big giant apology to

God. God is not looking for an empty apology. This word means a change of mind, a change of heart, and a change of direction.

The power of repentance is in the fact that from it comes real change. Jesus wanted them to repent because true repentance brings true change. The door to change is opened with the key of repentance.

Jesus wanted them to return. He instructed them to do their first works again. Sometimes the catalyst for moving forward is found in going back—back to worship, back to prayer, back to love, and back to life.

> The power of repentance is in the fact
> that from it comes real change.

I encourage you in Jesus's name not to leave your first love! Don't become spellbound by anything the enemy brings against you to distance you from the Lord. Break every spell of the enemy by remembering, repenting, and returning afresh to Jesus. Purpose at this very moment that you will never break the heart of Jesus by becoming a runaway bride.

Chapter 9

The POWER POSITION

Y OU HAVE WORLD-CHANGING, HELL-WRECKING, LIFE-transforming power at your disposal right this very moment. There is no way to overestimate the potential that lies in prayer.

No greater weapon in spiritual warfare is available to us than prayer. Prayer can break each and every spell of hell. We need to pray understanding that prayer is not just a defensive weapon; it's our secret weapon. Prayer is the equivalent of a nuclear bomb against the devil's kingdom.

Satan does not fear us when we go to church or conferences. He doesn't fear us when we read books, watch Christian television, or listen to CDs and DVDs of Bible teaching. Satan trembles when we pray.

Prayer is so disruptive and damaging to the kingdom of darkness, and this is why we must pray. The true power position in the life of every believer is the prayer position.

Jesus talked often about prayer, and not only did He talk about prayer, but He also prayed. Listen to His words in the Gospel of Matthew.

> And when you pray, you shall not be like the hypocrites.
> For they love to pray standing in the synagogues and on
> the corners of the streets, that they may be seen by men.
> Assuredly, I say to you, they have their reward. But you,
> when you pray, go into your room, and when you have

> shut your door, pray to your Father who is in the secret place; and your Father who sees in secret will reward you openly. And when you pray, do not use vain repetitions as the heathen do. For they think that they will be heard for their many words. Therefore do not be like them. For your Father knows the things you have need of before you ask Him.
>
> —MATTHEW 6:5–8

Notice the directness of His words in verse 5: "When you pray." Not if, but when. Jesus assumes that we would pray. If we believe that power, breakthrough, and intimacy with God are obtained through prayer, then it is illogical not to pray.

We are to be people of prayer. Our victory can only come through prayer. More than we need another conference, workshop, or special meeting, we need to pray. We must stop seeking after some formula for victory that espouses "Ten Steps to Breakthrough" or "Five Steps to Overcoming." How about this: one step to breakthrough, and that step is prayer!

Direct, definite, determined, disciplined, and desperate prayer is what we need. That is the power that will:

- Restore your marriage
- Bring healing and hope
- Provide for your needs
- Bring revival
- Save your lost loved ones
- Build our new facilities
- Bring joy over depression
- Free you from the shackles of the past
- Turn a has-been into a Holy Roller

Victory and power are both undeniably linked to prayer. The more you pray, the more power and victory you will experience. When you have an anemic prayer life, you will experience an anemic spiritual life.

God expects you and me to pray; prayer is the pediatrics of your relationship with Christ. Remember what Jesus declared to His followers. He said, "When you pray"—not *if*, but *when*! *When* is defined as a predetermined time, an ongoing activity. Prayer that brings power must be an ongoing reality in and of our lives. It should be something that is to be woven into the very fabric and fiber of who we are. Prayer for our spiritual life is as necessary as food is for our bodies.

Every church in the world should be a:

- Giving church
- Soul-winning church
- Spell-breaking church
- Devil-defeating church
- Excited church
- Worshipping church
- Missions-minded church
- Holy church
- Hungry church
- Healing church
- Growing, going, glowing church

But a church will never, ever be any of these things unless it becomes a praying church. I have pastored our church for almost fifteen years. We have seen indescribable victories and break-throughs. We have grown a core group of believers to a family of thousands committed to touching the world for Jesus. And prayer was the key.

Every single solitary victory of my life and ministry is undeniably linked to prayer. To really experience the fullness that God has for you, you must be willing to pray. Do you need a breakthrough in any area of your life? *You will never break through until you pray through!* I truly believe that a life that is marked by prayer is a life that is marked for miracles.

> Continue earnestly in prayer, being vigilant in it with thanksgiving.
> —Colossians 4:2

Pay close attention to Paul's instructions; don't just start to pray or pray once in a while, but start and then continue in prayer. The answer for your every issue is found in prayer. The Greek word for *continue* in this scripture, *proskartereo*, is an awesome word. It means to adhere to, be devoted to, give unremitting care to, and to persevere and not faint.

We pray when we are seeing results, and we pray when nothing is working. We pray when we are broke, and we pray when we are blessed. We pray when family situations are ideal, and we pray when our families are struggling. Prayer must be a continued constant for a Christian.

Prayer Warriors Stay in the Fight

True prayer warriors are devoted to the work of prayer. They understand that the power to break hell's spells are realized through prayer. They know what it is to be tenacious and determined to seek after the heart and face of God.

Prayer is not so much about defeating the devil as it is discovering God. The more time we spend with the Lord, the more we know Him. The more we know Him, the greater power we have over the devil's work. Prayer warriors are winners.

YOU CAN'T FRONT GOD

> And when you pray, you shall not be like the hypocrites.
> For they love to pray standing in the synagogues and on
> the corners of the streets, that they may be seen by men.
> Assuredly, I say to you, they have their reward.
> —MATTHEW 6:5

Don't fake folks get on your last nerve? Someone who is "phony baloney" is a challenge to tolerate in and out of the church. Hypocrites do more to hinder the work of the Lord than almost anything else. Obviously hypocrites aggravated Christ as well, because here in Matthew 6, He called them out. *Hupokrites*, the Greek word for *hypocrite*, is defined as an actor, a stage player, a pretender, or someone who wears a mask. Wow! A hypocrite is an actor, a stage player, and a performer. We don't need performers in the kingdom; we need worshippers.

We worship. He performs.

The Bible says hypocrites pray to be seen and heard. That kind of prayer is powerless, and when they have finished, they have their reward. Their reward is the stroking of their spiritual ego. When prayer is nothing less or nothing more than a staged show, it cannot bring about change.

Fake prayer yields no real answers.

In the company of others as well as alone with God, who is the hypocrite fooling? We cannot impress God with our verbiage and eloquent speech. He doesn't expect us to use big flashy words or pray in the language of the King James Version!

Never forget; there is nothing wrong with desperate prayers. Prayers that are prayed in hunger and need that cause us to cry out to God can be the most powerful of all.

Sometimes we just have to break it on down! When we are truly desperate for a breakthrough, and we really desire to defeat the devil, we will remove our masks. There is absolutely no way we will ever be able to front God anyway. He always knows what's under the mask, so it pays to be real.

> Therefore the LORD said: "Inasmuch as these people draw near with their mouths and honor Me with their lips, but have removed their hearts far from Me, and their fear toward Me is taught by the commandment of men…"
>
> —ISAIAH 29:13

Removed here in this text means to distance and widen the space between. God was saying that these people are talking a good game, but they are far from Him. Talk is cheap. God wants more than lip service, and He requires more than just noise. We must never mistake noise for revival.

God looks at the heart, and He sends revival and breakthrough to hungry hearts. Our prayers are not meant for the ears of men but for the ears of God.

IF GOD HEARS YOU, IT REALLY DOESN'T MATTER WHO ELSE HEARS YOU!

> But you, when you pray, go into your room, and when you have shut your door, pray to your Father who is in the secret place; and your Father who sees in secret will reward you openly.
>
> —MATTHEW 6:6

Jesus says we should pray in secret. Now this doesn't negate, nor does it cancel out, the power of praying together. What this means is that we should not pray to be seen or seek to impress others.

There's something very powerful that often happens when we really start praying. When we really start praying, especially about ourselves, we begin to whisper—at least I do! We all have issues we don't want anybody to know about but Jesus. This is why we should never pray with a mask on; He knows it all anyway! Just confess it. When you pray, *pray about it all*—pray about your issues, your struggles, and anything else. Don't be ashamed to share with Him what He already knows!

Pray about your pain, about what is making you want to quit, about your past, and everything else you are believing Him for. If you struggle with addiction or self-doubt, pray about it. But pray for Him to hear you. The Bible says He who sees in secret will reward you openly. (See Matthew 6:4, 6, and 18.) *Openly* appears three times in this chapter. That is the equivalent of an exclamation point in the Greek language that this text was originally written in. *Openly* means that we will be rewarded in an apparent and shining way.

In other words, Jesus is saying, "When I do this for you, everybody will know that it was My supernatural power that accomplished it." When the Lord delivers your child, restores your marriage, rebuilds your broken life, meets your financial need, or anything else you could not do, it will be obvious that He did it!

God will move, needs will be met, and Satan will be defeated in your life when you pray. Nothing moves until God moves, and God moves when you pray.

PRAYER, THE GREAT MIND MENDER

One of the most effective ways to strengthen and fortify your mind is through the power of prayer.

> Be careful for nothing; but in every thing by prayer and supplication with thanksgiving let your requests be made known unto God.
> —PHILIPPIANS 4:6, KJV

One of the most important realities relative to overcoming the enemy is to use the power of prayer. In prayer we discover resolve to persevere until we see results! Prayer is the place where not only is the mind mended but also the mind is made up as well. You have no greater weapon in your arsenal of spiritual weapons than prayer.

It blasts apart and devastates the kingdom of darkness; it is Satan's greatest fear and will cause you to be his overcoming foe!

When Paul penned these words in Philippians 4:6, he was actually in prison. He was experiencing monumental pressure, but he never let that pressure rob him of his prayer life. Paul had a real and true understanding of the unlimited power of prayer! He did not believe there was anything that could hinder his ability to pray and experience results. Prayer should not be contained just to a church gathering or a certain time or place during your day. It's good and wise to have a set time and a set place to meet God. But prayer is not about location; it's about habitation. Prayer is about meeting with God, and God will meet you anytime you seek Him.

I have my set time and place for prayer, but I can also pray anywhere—and have done so. I have become burdened before in public places and dropped my head, closed my eyes, and silently prayed through to an incredible encounter with the Lord.

God met Paul in jail, and He will meet you at your job—or anywhere else for that matter. Prayer is always ideal even when the place is not.

THE POWER POSITION

Prayer is powerful! There is no way to know all that prayer has accomplished throughout the centuries. Lives have been saved, wars have been averted, catastrophes have been canceled, and Satan's plans have been frustrated through the power of prayer.

I want to share with you three types of powerful prayer. Chances are you have prayed each of these even when you didn't know it.

1. The power of petition

When we pray prayers of petition, we are simply asking of God. Petitioning prayer is requesting God to meet our personal needs, wants, and desires.

This is the level of prayer we are most familiar with, and without a doubt this is an absolutely necessary part of the true believer's prayer life. No matter what you have, you don't have it all, and no matter who you are, you need God. There are elements of life that are completely out of our control, and in those moments we petition God.

The Lord dealt with me awhile back about the fact that I didn't have to operate in less than what He has made available to and for me. I began to wonder what I might not be experiencing because I didn't have the guts to ask.

Now I am incredibly grateful for all God has done in my life, and I am so blessed. But there are things that I want to do for Him, but I need Him to do it! I am trusting God for more facilities to touch the homeless and the hungry and to make a greater impact for the gospel's sake around the world. But I had to realize I need to ask! What are we missing out on within the body of Christ because we simply have not asked?

Asking does not offend God.

> Ye have not, because ye ask not.
> —JAMES 4:2, KJV

Realize that God is not upset when we petition and ask of Him. Our relationship with God is based on more than just what we ask of Him, but there is asking involved. I believe it is time to begin as never before to ask God for big things!

It's time to ask! Ask God for what you need. Ask God for financial breakthroughs. Ask God for revival. Ask Him for healing. Even as you are reading this book, stop and ask! After you ask, just trust the Lord that He has heard. James said we don't have because we don't ask.

The word *because* in the Book of James means on account of, for this reason, or to avoid. Don't miss out on your promises from God because you have avoided asking! Don't miss your mighty moment because you didn't ask!

Jesus Himself tells us to ask.

> Ask, and it will be given to you; seek, and you will find; knock, and it will be opened to you. For everyone who asks receives, and he who seeks finds, and to him who knocks it will be opened.
>
> —MATTHEW 7:7–8

You may be thinking, "I did ask; God just didn't answer!" But you need to obtain a clear understanding of the text. From the original language of the New Testament, the words *ask*, *seek*, and *knock* imply a continuance. They mean to keep asking, keep seeking, and keep knocking.

Don't miss out on your promises from God because you have avoided asking!

Don't give up; ask until you see results! Pursue Him. God responds to those who pursue Him. Prayer will fortify your mind. As long as you're asking, your mind is occupied with expectancy. I'm not trying to paint a picture of a God that is a celestial sugar daddy. I believe we need to have balance in everything.

But I do what Paul recorded in the Book of Romans. I "call those things that be not as though they were!" (See Romans 4:17, KJV.) I confess, pray, and ask of God. I speak in faith, trusting in God's mighty hand all the way through the process.

Call your family saved, your needs met, and your breakthrough manifested in faith. Our word *petition* actually originates from the Latin, and when you break it down, it means to aim at and to lay claim to. Aim, ask, and claim your miracle in Jesus's name!

Say it until you see it!

Get the mind of God, and say it until you see it. Ask Him to help you to pray His mind and His will for your life. As I have matured in the Lord, my asking has changed. I still ask, but I ask differently. I believe in asking God for His blessings. But over the years I have begun to find myself asking "God, make me" a whole lot more than "God, give me."

You must not miss your miracle because you grew tired of asking. God wants you to ask.

> Ask of Me, and I will give You the nations for Your inheritance, and the ends of the earth for Your possession.
> —PSALM 2:8

It's time as never before to ask in faith believing! Now, petition is so important. However, petition often involves circumstances and personal needs, which leads me to the next type of prayer: intercession.

2. *The power of intercession*

Intercession often concerns people, and people are priceless! One of the greatest examples of intercession that brought results is found when the first martyr of the church, Stephen, was killed. Stephen had a glorious obsession with the cause of Christ. He cared more about that cause than anything else in the world.

> …and cast him out of the city, and stoned him: and the witnesses laid down their clothes at a young man's feet, whose name was Saul. And they stoned Stephen, calling upon God, and saying, Lord Jesus, receive my spirit. And he kneeled down, and cried with a loud voice, Lord, lay not this sin to their charge. And when he had said this, he fell asleep.
> —ACTS 7:58–60, KJV

Stephen raises a prayer of intercession for the band of murdering religious fanatics who took his life. His final prayer was a cry of intercession for God's mercy upon his murderers. Among them was a young man and the reason for Stephen's prayer. This young man was none other than Saul of Tarsus.

Did this prayer of intercession work? Yes! The entire world has been mightily affected by the power of Stephen's prayer! I believe it was the power of intercessory prayer that turned murdering Saul into preaching Paul! Revival, the salvation of lost souls, and much more are unlocked through the power of intercession!

The definition for the word *intercession* is a powerful one.

> **Intercession**—to entreat for favor, to stand in and represent someone. To stand in the gap!

Intercession is the work of intervention. When we intercede, we stand in the place of someone and represent them. We pray and seek God as earnestly as if we were praying for ourselves. Intercessors are gap people.

God has called each of us to stand in the gap, to intervene and intercede for others. In the Book of Hebrews Christ gives us the greatest example of intercession.

> Therefore He is also able to save to the uttermost those who come to God through Him, since He always lives to make intercession for them.
> —HEBREWS 7:25

Prayer like this is a selfless prayer. We are like Christ when we operate in intercessory prayer. As Christians we are called to love, and one of the greatest examples of loving another is through intercessory prayer! When we intercede for another, there becomes an element of strong compassion that takes over. We experience an uncommon desire for another's breakthrough to be realized. *Compassion* is a powerful word in the Greek.

> **Compassion**—to yearn from your inner being to minister, to be stirred in and from the depth of oneself!

Eight times in the New Testament Jesus was moved with compassion. Crowds, money, and applause didn't move Christ. He wasn't moved by worldly recognition, fame, or anything of the sort. Compassion moved Jesus! He was moved with compassion, and He healed, He fed, He preached, and He bled.

Compassionate intercession wreaks havoc upon the devil's kingdom. Whom do you need to intervene for? Who is counting on your intercessory prayer for their deliverance? Allow the Lord to show you, and then become a gap person who prayerfully intercedes for others.

Supplication—praying with urgency

> Confess your trespasses to one another, and pray for one another, that you may be healed. The effective, fervent prayer of a righteous man avails much.
> —JAMES 5:16

An accurate definition for the word *prayer* here is supplication. The Bible says this type of prayer avails. When you avail, you win, so supplication is a winning prayer. Supplication means to pray with a sense of urgency. It means to pray with deep concern. It's prayer accompanied by a burden, something you need God to give His immediate attention to.

Much of the church has lost its sense of urgency. In many instances we don't pray, preach, or witness with a sense of urgency. Hell operates every day with a sense of urgency; God have mercy, but much of the church has lost its desperation in prayer!

At some point we need to know what it is to become desperate in our prayer and pursuit of God. Desperate people are different from everyone else. I am penning these words at thirty-five thousand feet. I have been in a season of relentless ministry and responsibility. But even as I sit here in this plane writing these words, I am realizing I am a desperate man.

I am desperate for a move of God that will bring an awakening of salvation to our sin-sick world. I am desperate to see young people lay down their lives for the cause of Christ and live Jesus before their peers. I am desperate to see hurting people helped, hungry people fed, and broken people mended.

Yes, I am. I am desperate.

Jesus Himself had a sense of urgency when He was on Planet Earth.

> Who, in the days of His flesh, when He had offered up prayers and supplications, with vehement cries and tears to Him who was able to save Him from death.
> —HEBREWS 5:7

The church must regain her sense of urgency, and you and I must pray with urgency. Never forget; hell has a sense of urgency. We are on dangerous ground if we allow hell to operate with a greater passion and motivation than we do.

Jesus prayed with a sense of urgency. Jesus knew something most of the church knows little of, and that is desperate supplication! This is very intense, but the power of urgent supplication can break to pieces every one of hell's spells!

We are on dangerous ground if we allow hell to operate with a greater passion and motivation than we do.

When we pray with urgency, we are not praying in fear or dread; we are praying urgently in faith and expectancy. Allow the Lord to birth in you an urgency for prayer and supplication. Satan fears us when we begin to operate with a sense of urgency.

Travail—energy put into prayer

Anyone who experiences great victories in his or her life understands travail. Students, athletes, and successful people all comprehend travail. Availing prayer and travailing prayer walk hand in hand, because there are times that the only way we will avail is if we are willing to travail.

Travail speaks of the process of birthing. When a woman is going to bring a new life into the world, she must travail to do so. Are you willing to travail in prayer and birth the next season of power in your life? The things you're trusting God for may require you to travail in prayer. Even when it is hard, are you willing to travail and never give up?

The pain of birthing is the price of birthing.

Some of the breakthroughs you're trusting God for will only be birthed through the process, pain, and price of travail. Travail can mean praying in pain and believing in brokenness. When we travail in prayer, we press through the hard and difficult seasons, and we are poised for the miraculous. Travailing prayer reflects intensity and how bad you want a thing!

> Therefore I say to you, whatever things you ask when you pray, believe that you receive them, and you will have them.
> —MARK 11:24

Desire is defined as a deep-seated craving, an intense longing for attainment. It's not some casual thing you can live with or without. When you get ready to travail, you will not be denied. It is very hard to believe someone is desperate for a thing when they refuse to pray!

Prayer is a vocal expression of what you desire.

Supplication is urgency placed into prayer, and travail is energy! Travailing prayer is determined prayer. It's when you make up your mind not to give up, no matter what!

What have you made up your mind about? What are you trusting

God for that you have not seen as of yet? I want to encourage you, never give up! Travail, even if you aren't seeing what you want to see. Keep praying, keep declaring, and keep praying. Don't give up on that son or daughter. Don't quit on that lost loved one. Don't throw in the towel on your dream of ministry or financial security. Keep believing!

A delayed blessing does not mean a denied one; it's time to travail! Fortify your mind; strengthen your mind, yourself, and your resolve through prayer. Don't be denied. Be encouraged and travail!

PRAYER IS THE POWER POSITION

You are exercising your greatest authority over hell's spells when you pray. You will never have greater power than prayer power. Prayer power is greater than any power known to man and is the highest call of a Christian. Prayer is your right, your privilege, and your duty.

> Let the priests, who minister to the LORD, weep between the porch and the altar; let them say, "Spare Your people, O LORD, and do not give Your heritage to reproach, that the nations should rule over them. Why should they say among the peoples, 'Where is their God?'"
>
> —JOEL 2:17

The Old Testament high priest wore an ephod with two onyx stones on the shoulders. On these stones were carved the names of the twelve tribes of Israel. The priest would petition God as well as offer prayers of supplication. He would travail and intercede on behalf of his people. This was his solemn duty as priest.

And because of our connection to Jesus, now you and I are priests unto the Lord. Peter understood this fact and called us just that.

> But you are a chosen generation, a royal priesthood.
>
> —1 PETER 2:9

We must fortify our minds and assume our role as the royal priesthood! Assume the power position, and you will break the power of hell's spells and experience victory in Jesus's name in your life!

Chapter 10

The SPELLBOUND HOME

THERE IS NO PLACE LIKE HOME.

I love going home. To me, home is my happy place. I am blessed to do life and ministry with some of the greatest people a guy could ever hope for. I have many deep and abiding relationships, and I feel fortunate to lead an incredible life-giving church. I hang out with people who share my same passion for changing the world with the love of Jesus. My days are busy and intense, and sometimes my responsibilities seem overwhelming. So when it's time to go home, I'm a happy man.

I have three precious kids and a wife whose outer beauty is only surpassed by her inner beauty. My family is amazing, and I am thankful. I don't want to be redundant, but I will say it again: there is no place like home.

As much as I have realized that fact, I have come to know something. Satan has a keen understanding of that as well. This is why he reserves his most intense attacks for the family. He knows if he can sabotage the family, he has dealt a crippling blow to God's plan for everyone connected to it.

WHO'S IN CHARGE?

Satan wants control of your home, and he will do anything to have it. Many homes in America are occupied by families who have been unknowingly spellbound by the enemy. Don't get me wrong; they are good people, but nevertheless Satan is intensely at work in their midst. His tactics are sinister and covert. He has used his tricks of the trade for so long that most people are oblivious to his tactics.

Until now.

Satan must be exposed if he is ever to be expelled. You may be sitting here reading this book at this very moment wondering how on earth does a home become spellbound. You don't need to think of it as a witch or a soothsayer casting spells and reciting incantations against your family. Satan is far more subtle than that.

The root of Satan's power in the home is the same as it is everywhere else. The root of Satan's power is always rebellion.

To be partially obedient is to be disobedient.

A working definition for the word *rebellion* is the attempted or enforced use of illegitimate authority. And it happens all the time in the home.

> For rebellion is as the sin of witchcraft, and stubbornness
> is as iniquity and idolatry. Because you have rejected the
> word of the LORD, He also has rejected you.
> —1 SAMUEL 15:23

This particular scripture was directed at King Saul because of his disobedience to the Lord. Saul had been instructed by the Lord to contend with the Amalekites for their ruthlessness against Israel. Saul was instructed to slay the people and all their livestock. Nothing was to be left of them. After warning the Kenites (who had been allies and friends of Israel) to flee, Saul launched an attack against the Amalekites. He utterly defeated them and took King Agag hostage.

Instead of walking in total obedience to God, Saul did what he thought was best. He spared Agag and kept the best of the livestock.

Saul followed God's plan but not all the way. To be partially obe-dient is to be disobedient.

It didn't matter that he did part of what God said or even most of what God said; he had to do all of what God said to do. This story gives us a very clear picture of how Satan can cause a family to become spellbound. Let me share with you some illustrations and show you how Satan can take control of the home through rebellion.

CHILD'S PLAY OR REBELLION?

Little Tiffany is as cute as a button and the apple of her parents' eye. She is a handful, to say the least. She's not just a five-year-old beauty queen; she's a five-year-old drama queen. She is as sweet as sugar—as long as things are going her way. But if she doesn't get her way, look out!

One afternoon her mom picks her up from school, and little Tiffany wants to know what was for supper that night. Her Mom braces herself and says, "Why, Tiffany, we are having baked chicken, rice, and broccoli. Doesn't that sound yummy?"

Tiffany lets out a cry and says, "Yuck! I don't want that. I want pizza! Order me some pizza!"

Mom replies sternly, "No, young lady, we are having chicken, and that's that!"

Well, in that moment all hell breaks loose. Tiffany screams, yells, and pitches an absolute fit. Her mom desperately tries to quiet her down but to no avail. "I want pizza. I hate you, Mom. You never give me what I want. *I want pizza!*"

Her mom is tired from a long day and just is not up for the fight. To keep the peace, mom picks up the phone and dials the pizza restaurant. This scenario plays over and over again in this family. Guess what? Somebody is spellbound, and it's not Tiffany. Tiffany is being rebellious; she is claiming illegitimate authority over her mom. Not only is she claiming it, she is also obtaining it.

> Rebellion is as the sin of witchcraft.
> —1 SAMUEL 15:23

Children cannot be allowed to exercise illegitimate authority in the home; that's rebellion. And God calls rebellion witchcraft. Children must learn to obey.

> Children, obey your parents in the Lord, for this is right. "Honor your father and mother," which is the first commandment with promise.
> —EPHESIANS 6:1–2

I want to bring to light two words Paul used in this scripture concerning children. First he said obey. *Obey* here means to listen, hearken, and submit to the authority of the parents. Children must learn to obey and walk in submission to their parents. I know this is conceptually challenging nowadays, but the truth is the truth, and it must be told. If you and I don't teach our children to obey, law enforcement will.

As a Christian parent you are the law at your house.

The next word I want to highlight from Paul's teaching is *honor*, which leads to our next story.

THE HONOR OF HONORING

Johnny is fourteen and has it all. He lives in a nice home with a great family. He has all the latest in video gaming equipment, a laptop, and an endless supply of almost anything he wants.

Not only does he *have* it all, but he also *knows* it all.

At fourteen Johnny knows everything—or at least he thinks he does. He's not really a bad kid; he just has his own opinions—about everything! Johnny is out of school for the summer, and his dad thinks it's time for him to learn some responsibility and do something other than play video games all the time. So his dad leaves him a couple of chores to do. Johnny is to mow the grass and wash the car and, as Dad said, "Do a real good job."

Johnny figures that these things are certainly not his responsibility, but he will appease his dad by just doing at least one of the jobs. So he hastily washes the car before lunch and calls it quits. The car is not really clean because Johnny doesn't put forth much effort.

His dad comes in from work and finds Johnny playing a video game. The yard is not mowed and the car looks awful. Dad questions why. Johnny responds, "Well, Dad, maybe I didn't mow the grass, but I did wash the car. In my opinion that's pretty good! It's hot out there, and you ought to be happy I did that much!"

Johnny's dad thinks a minute and replies, "Well, you know, son, good job washing the car! Maybe next time you can actually get it clean. And who knows? Maybe one day you will be able to fit mowing the grass in." But remember, to be partially obedient is to be disobedient.

Ask Saul.

It's still rebellion. Paul said in Ephesians 6 that children should obey and honor their parents. *Honor* means to respect, give attention to, and walk in full obedience. It is an honorable thing for children to honor their parents. Parents are spellbound if they feel they need to debate with their children and "give in" on issues in order to maintain peace.

We love our children, and part of loving them is teaching them to walk in complete obedience to what is the good and proper authority in their lives. Never forget: opinionated, excuse-making children turn into opinionated, excuse-making adults.

Let's take a look at our next household.

THE CONTROL FREAK

Jeff has been married to Joan for five years. Though Jeff's mother does not actually live in the house with Jeff and Joan, she is still very involved with their relationship. Jeff has always been a momma's boy. He is afraid to make one decision without consulting Momma, and that's the way Momma likes it. Fear is a major weapon in the arsenal of a control freak.

No matter what Joan does, it's never good enough. Mom judges Joan harshly and has the final say-so in her son's marriage. If there is an argument or a decision that has to be made, Jeff always consults his mom. Poor Jeff, he can't do anything without Momma. This places an incredible strain on their marriage. Joan loves Jeff, but every day Jeff shows where his heart really is. Joan is growing weary of the fight and is ready to call it quits.

Mom's in charge, Joan is tired, and Jeff is spellbound.

You must admit it's a little freaky for a grown man to still be that dominated by his mother. Jesus spoke about marriage in the Gospel of Matthew and addresses this situation head-on. His words are very telling to a man or woman who has a control freak parent.

> For this cause shall a man leave father and mother, and
> shall cleave to his wife.
> —MATTHEW 19:5, KJV

For marriage to work Jesus said there would have to be some leaving and some cleaving—whether Momma likes it or not! In this context the word *leave* means to become loosened. The only real hope for the marriage that is bound and shackled by a controlling spirit is for the one who is spellbound to be loosened by the power of God.

Jesus said to leave. Leave the control; leave the domination; leave the bondage.

Don't war with your family, but show the controlling spirit that it does not control you. Jesus said to cleave to your mate. Cleave means, essentially, to join to and to stick with. Stick to your mate like glue and build your lives together.

If you are reading this and you're realizing that you have been trying to control your married child's life, you must take authority over a controlling spirit. The authority you haven been trying to have is not yours. This is improper authority and is rebellion. And God calls rebellion witchcraft. You must stop trying to dominate your child's marriage and let that child leave. They will never cleave if you won't let them leave.

The controlling spirit is not limited to a parental situation within the family. There are several ways the controlling spirit can and will manifest.

THE CHOKER

Bill and Mary have been married for years. Bill is a hard worker and a good provider. Mary has had a great job in the past but decided to become a stay-at-home mom while the kids were in school.

Because Mary is not working an outside job (although she certainly is working), Bill has come to think of himself as the guy who brings in the dough, so he is in charge. He feels like he should decide where every dollar is spent. What he says goes, and there is to be no discussion in the matter.

Mary is not allowed to have friends outside the house, and Bill gets furious if she wants to do something without him. Bill comes home and immediately begins barking orders and dominates everything that goes on in the house. The kids are fearful of Dad, and Mary is intimidated. Bill continually reminds everyone of how hard he works and the fact that he is in charge.

The person who is truly in charge rarely has to declare it.

Bill angrily dominates the entire family unit. He chokes the joy out of the house, and Mary feels like she is being smothered every day. There is no viewpoint allowed in the family except for Bill's, and he has even gone so far to say, "If you don't like it, leave!"

Mary is choking, the kids are afraid, Bill is railing, and the home is spellbound.

If you are a husband or a wife and you verbally or physically abuse your family, there's a spell on your home. If you try to control the members of your family through hateful actions and harsh words, there's a devil loose. If your house is fear-filled, something is dreadfully wrong.

> There is no fear in love; but perfect love casts out all fear.
> —1 JOHN 4:18

Your home should be love-filled rather than fear-filled. The word *fear* here in this scripture is the Greek word *phobos*. We see in this word our English word *phobia*. You are being controlled by the enemy if your family has a phobia, and that phobia is you.

Perfect love casts out all fear.

Chokers kill the love, peace, and joy in their own homes. If you're a choker and feel as if you must rule everything with an iron fist, repent and ask God to help you. Renounce rebellion in your own life, because if you use authority wrongly or illegitimately, you're being rebellious. Lead in love and not through control.

Controlling, choking people often wind up alone.

THE GUILT-TRIPPER

Shelly has always been needy. Although she has raised two children and been married to the same man for thirty years, nobody connected to her can really be happy. The reason? Shelly is a guilt-tripper.

Anytime her husband, Ed, wants to go hang out with the guys or go fishing or watch a game, Shelly starts. "You just don't love me anymore. You never want to spend time with me. You always want to get away from me."

Be very careful when you use words like *never* and *always* when you are disagreeing with someone you love.

Ed feels guilty every time he wants to do something alone or with other friends. He constantly finds himself trying to measure up to Shelly's wants, needs, and desires. He is frustrated because he feels as if he cannot.

A home can't be built in an atmosphere of guilt.

Shelly wants the kids and grandkids around her all the time. She can't stand it if her kids spend time with their mates' families. She says things like, "I guess you just love them more than us. What Dad and I provided for you was just not good enough. The grandkids would probably rather be with them anyway. You know, I'm not going to be around forever." That is classic guilt-tripper language.

A home can't be built in an atmosphere of guilt. The devil wants us to think that this behavior is really no big deal. But this is some of the worst manipulation of all. These are some of the most oppressive and bondage-producing actions a family member can engage in. To control through guilt is tragic. When someone constantly tries to manipulate you with the power of guilt, you try to avoid them as much as possible.

It's human nature to seek out a blesser and not an oppressor. And God despises the oppressive, controlling spirit.

> [God] will break in pieces the oppressor.
> —PSALM 72:4

Oppression is a cruel and illegitimate use of authority, no matter how it's packaged. The family that is controlled by a guilt-tripper is a miserable bunch, and that power must be broken. If you see those tendencies in yourself, come against them in the name of Jesus.

It's time for you to develop a sense of peace and freedom. The day that a guilt-tripper is released from this negative behavior is a victorious day for everyone. The family walks in liberty, and the guilt-tripper is able to finally realize, "My family loves me, my friends love me, and most of all, yes, Jesus loves me!"

THE TOLL OF CONTROL

There are many ways a controlling spirit can enter into a family and cause them to be spellbound. Whether a man uses masculinity, bravado, or money, or a woman uses fussing, guilt, or sex, it is wrong to try to control others. Your relationships should not be control-filled but love-filled.

Love based on control is not love at all.

When someone in the family has a controlling spirit that keeps the family in bondage, that home is spellbound. If you recognize those attributes in someone you love or even in yourself, it's time to overcome that controlling spirit in Jesus's name.

Remember, God is on your side, and He is for your family. You are not wrestling or fighting flesh and blood, but this is a spiritual fight. Be encouraged, claim God's power of freedom, and break the power of every spell in your home.

> Stand fast therefore in the liberty by which Christ has made us free, and do not be entangled again with a yoke of bondage.
> —GALATIANS 5:1

Every one of hell's spells can and must be broken. God has designed liberty for you and your family. Christ desires for you and your family to be free! In Jesus's name don't bring the people you love into controlling bondage. Refuse to be held captive yourself. You are a *spell breaker* in Jesus's name!

Chapter 11

GENERATIONAL CURSES

THE CONCEPT OF GENERATIONAL CURSES IS ONE OF THE most intense and thought-provoking concepts in all of Christian theology. This topic has been rarely taught. Unfortunately, when it has, it's often been mishandled by well-meaning but errant teachers. No matter what subject is taught from the Bible, ultimately that teaching should feed our faith and starve our fear. Anytime we hear a message, no matter what the subject, there must be hope somewhere in it.

A message on hell should remind us of God's grace and the promise of heaven. A message revolving around trials should awaken in us the reality of our deliverer. When we speak of God's judgment, we should also be aware of God's mercy to those He has redeemed. God would rather forgive us than judge us.

So as I address generational curses, I don't want you to think of God as some cosmic creator who is waiting in the wings looking for the first chance to curse you and your family. Through the power of Christ God is not a curser but a blesser. Jesus did not come to curse and condemn us; He came to love and liberate us.

> For God did not send His Son into the world to condemn the world, but that the world through Him might be saved.
>
> —JOHN 3:17

Jesus didn't come to condemn the world, because the world was already condemned. Jesus came to save it.

> God would rather forgive us than judge us.

Generational curses are a reality. If you don't believe that, just look around you. Have you ever seen a family that seems to be plagued by certain sins or certain issues? Alcoholism, drug addiction, divorce, sexual bondage, anger, depression, sickness, and more—and that's only the tip of the iceberg. Statistics tell us that these issues are often passed from one generation to the next with devastating effects.

This is what the Bible speaks of in the Book of Exodus.

> You shall not make for yourself a carved image, or any likeness of anything that is in heaven above, or that is in the earth beneath, or that is in the water under the earth; you shall not bow down to them nor serve them. For I, the LORD your God, am a jealous God, visiting the iniquity of the fathers on the children to the third and fourth generations of those who hate Me, but showing mercy to thousands, to those who love Me and keep My commandments.
> —EXODUS 20:4–6

It is obvious as you read this scripture that generational curses are certainly a reality and have been so since the fall of man. Our understanding of this term is usually far different from the biblical reality. When we think of a curse, we think of a hex or bad luck placed on a person or a family. To some, when they think of a curse, they think of something they read in a fairy-tale book. Remember the princess who was placed under a curse and fell into a deep sleep?

Some people feel that they have to wear a religious symbol (like a cross) because if they don't, they're in danger of being cursed. Many saved and blood-bought believers walk in considerable fear because they think there are legions of demons that have the ability to curse them whenever they desire to. This is totally wrong!

Don't Confuse Punishment With Iniquity

Another wrong way of thinking as it relates to generational curses is that God is punishing one generation for the sins of another. This also is complete falsehood. It is possible to suffer because of the sins of your parents, but does suffering denote punishment from God? Exodus 34:7 does not say that God visited the punishment of the fathers to the children; it says "visiting the iniquity." Iniquity is sin. So what this scripture means is that children will repeat many of the same sins as their parents.

Parents possess incredible influence over their children.

With that being said, let's define the term *generational curse* in a simple and easy-to-understand fashion.

> **Generational curse**—the result of ingrained behavior patterns that are passed from one generation to the next

A generational curse is when we practice the sin of our forefathers and pass that behavior to our children. A generational curse does not manifest out of nowhere. If there is a curse, then there's a cause.

> A curse without cause shall not alight.
> —PROVERBS 26:2

Wherever a generational curse exists in a family, there is a reason for it. Our thinking is skewed, however, when we blame God for a generational curse. God is not the source of generational iniquity; man is. It would be like slicing a carrot and cutting your finger, and then blaming the knife. Sin is always our decision; it is never God's.

With sin there are always consequences. This is why the power of sin must be broken through the blood of Jesus.

A FAMILY TRADITION

Growing up I listened to every kind of music. My preferences were soul, rock, and R&B. However, being raised in the South meant I got a real good dose of country music as well. I remember a song I would hear blaring out on the radio from time to time by Hank Williams Jr. It was called "Family Tradition." The words to the song were very revealing as it relates to generational sins and struggles.

Hank Williams Jr. seems to describe his own personal behavior as it related to drinking, smoking, and other addictive issues in this old country song. His father (also a famous country singer) was said to have many of these same struggles also. Isn't it something that he calls this behavior "a family tradition."

Many times we label behaviors family traditions when they are actually generational curses. There are sinful acts that become a part of certain families. They become family traditions. There are familiar spirits that attach themselves to families and bring about much havoc. The word *familiar* originates from the Latin language. It is close to the word *family*. It actually means pertaining to family, or well acquainted with.

There are familiar spirits that seem to show up at family reunions and eat ribs with the rest of us! Just kidding; they don't eat ribs! But you do hear things like, "That's just Uncle John. He drinks a lot like his daddy and brothers do." Or, "She's just like her mom and grandmother. She has a real bad temper, but she can't help it." Or, "That's just the Jones way" or "the Brown way."

These are examples of a familiar spirit that has attached itself to a family. This spirit has been present so long in the family until destructive behavior is not only tolerated, but it's also expected.

You may be able to look at your family tree and see certain spiritual, physical, and emotional issues that have been present for generations. Even in my own life I have seen this reality. In the physical sense my family has struggled greatly with diabetes, high blood pressure, and many other physical ailments. I began to battle some of those same issues. I came to realize that it was directly related to our diet. Our way of eating had been passed down to us for generations, and it was killing us. So years ago I changed my eating habits and began to exercise. Thankfully that generational curse has been broken off my life.

The plan and desire of God is not for us to be cursed. He sent Jesus to liberate us and to set us free from each and every influence of demonic forces.

The Origin of Generational Curses

The origin of a generational curse is always, always sin. A generational curse is rooted in sin. The question is: How does a generational curse take root in the family? To answer that question requires us to have a clear understanding of sin. Now I know that sin is sin, but we kid ourselves if we don't think that there are different levels to sin.

To compare rape or murder to someone lying or cheating on a test is absolutely unthinkable. It's important to understand the different levels of sin, and through that understanding you will begin to have clarity concerning generational curses. Now sin is sin, and we know for sure that the wages of sin is death. But Jesus addressed our sin through His sacrifice on the cross.

> But He was wounded for our transgressions, He was bruised for our iniquities.... Yet it pleased the LORD to bruise Him...and make His soul an offering for sin.
> —ISAIAH 53:5, 10

The great news is that this scripture is a prophetic preview of the power that Jesus would exercise over sin through His death. But I want you to zero in on three realities here: sin, transgressions, and iniquities.

SIN IS MISSING THE MARK

A very simplified definition of sin means to miss the mark or come up short of the goal. Would you be willing to admit that at times you have missed the mark? When we miss the mark, we haven't measured up to what God is anticipating. Everyone has missed the mark, and none of us have lived our lives without error or sin.

> For all have sinned and fall short of the glory of God.
> —ROMANS 3:23

Falling short is not hitting the mark. That reality is present in each of our lives. This is why Jesus came. The Bible says that He was made an offering for our sin. Where we missed the mark, He did not. Because of that we are able to claim victory over sin. If you have missed the mark, there is no need for you to hang your head in despair and give up. Every mark on His body was made for every time you and I have missed the mark.

He was marked up for our mess-ups.

TRANSGRESSION IS GOING TOO FAR

The word *pesha* of the Old Testament is translated *transgression* and also *trespass*. *Trespass* means to violate and disregard established restrictions and boundaries. Simply put, transgression is the act of going too far. We can trespass against God and man. If someone owns a house or property and puts out a "No Trespassing" sign, whoever crosses onto that property is a trespasser. To trespass is to transgress. The owner of the property could demand the consequences of the transgression.

God has set certain boundaries for men and women to live within. When we operate outside of those boundaries, we transgress or trespass against God. We have all had times when we transgressed and went outside of God's boundaries. But thankfully we never went so far that His grace could not reach us.

> He was wounded for our transgressions.
> —ISAIAH 53:5

For every time you and I went too far, Jesus bore wounds. It doesn't matter how much we have transgressed. He was wounded for our transgressions. For every time we went too far, for every time we overstepped boundaries, Jesus was wounded.

Including His circumcision, Jesus bore wounds in seven places on His body. Seven is the number of rest in the Bible. God took six days to create the world and all that's in it, and on the seventh day He rested. There is rest in Jesus.

Claim rest in Jesus's name, and refuse to allow past transgressions the right to have any power over you. The devil would like to keep you wearied, worn, and worried over your past. But Jesus was wounded to give you rest. No more should you lose sleep over what was; Jesus took care of every transgression. So it's time to rest.

INIQUITY IS THE INNER STRUGGLE

The third level of sin is iniquity. *Iniquity* from the original Hebrew means perversity or depravity. Iniquity is sin that takes hold of a person's heart and speaks of the inner struggle a man has with sin.

It is sin that is practiced so much until it becomes a lifestyle. Iniquity is the root of a generational curse. The person that is controlled by iniquity develops a distortion of right and wrong. They are literally drawn toward certain behaviors, because iniquity is reigning strongly in their lives.

Iniquity can be addiction, violence, sexual sin, or anything else that is practiced over and over again until it takes root and gains control. This behavior can capture a person so thoroughly that it becomes a part of their very being. This iniquity can be passed down to his or her children and to generations beyond that.

Children can be born drawn toward certain types of behavior, and there's really no explanation for it in the natural. There is no natural explanation because it's not natural or chemical; it is spiritual. It seems that some people are born pulled toward certain behaviors.

Maybe you have wrestled with specific things in your own life and don't even know why. Even if you don't give in, you question the drawing you have toward certain sins. It could be gossip, pornography, anger, untruthfulness, addictions, adulterous thoughts, or any kind of sin you contend with.

Paul understood this and addressed it in 2 Thessalonians 2:7. He called it the "mystery of iniquity" (KJV). Paul paints a powerful picture of a generational curse. It is sin that a person is drawn toward and they don't even know why. It's the mystery of iniquity. Have you ever asked yourself, "Why do I do what I do? Why do I act a certain way or contend with some sins more than others?" Very often if you check past generations, you will identify those same struggles in your forefathers.

> You can stop any destructive behavior in your generation.

Iniquities are those things that boil up inside of us. They are our inner battles and issues. It can be something that nobody knows about but you, or it can just as easily be something that manifests clearly before everyone's eyes.

You owe it to those you love to deal with every generational curse that tries to attach itself to your life. If your mother was angry or addicted, you owe it to your mate and children to stop that generational curse dead in its tracks. If your father was verbally and physically abusive, the people in your life deserve you at your best. You can stop any destructive behavior in your generation.

There is not a single generational curse that cannot be broken off of your life and family. Remember, iniquities are inner issues. But Jesus covered all sin when He gave His life for us on the cross. Jesus addressed sin, trespasses, and iniquities when He was crucified.

> He was bruised for our iniquities.
>
> —ISAIAH 53:5

It is incredibly powerful to note that Jesus was bruised for a particular reason. He was bruised for our iniquities. What are bruises? Bruises are outer manifestations of inner bleedings. He was bruised for my iniquities, my inner sins, and inner issues.

Jesus bled on the inside for my inside struggles.

Jesus addressed it all at Calvary. He bled on the inside to bring victory for you on the inside! No sin or iniquity has power over you because Jesus bled so that you could be free! Those things that would like to boil up inside of you are brought into check by the bruising blood of Jesus.

While I am on the subject of the inner bleeding of Jesus, let me go a little farther. Even if you have been wounded on the inside, even if you are carrying inner hurts and inner pain, you can be free in Jesus's name! Maybe a parent, a mate, a family member, or even a stranger has wounded you. You may feel you've been cut so deep within that you don't know how you could ever heal. This may be a fact, but the truth is, you don't have to walk wounded.

Jesus bled on the inside for your inside wounds. Let that reality awaken in you. Jesus can arise at this very moment within you, with healing in His wings. He paid for it, and if you need it, it's yours. Not tomorrow, not next week, not next month, or next year— it's for you, and it's for now.

Eight Steps to New Beginnings!

This is your moment to realize that every generational curse can and must be broken—and not only broken but also reversed. It's time for iniquity to be destroyed. I have walked this process out in my own life. There was incredible violence, addiction, and mental illness in the generations that preceded me, but today I stand free. When I look at my own testimony, I understand the power of breaking generational curses. In Jesus's name, every generational curse has been broken off my life and my children.

Do you believe in new beginnings? I do. I love new beginnings! Isn't there something beautiful about fresh starts? Jesus specializes in providing tired old lives with brand-new beginnings. No matter what has plagued your past, Jesus has provided enough mercy for the moment to unleash a new life.

In biblical numerology the number eight represents new beginnings. There are eight simple steps to releasing the power in your life to break every generational curse. It's time to embrace the new season that lies before you.

1. Fully submit to God.

When we think of submission or surrender, we naturally equate it with losing. But in this case submission is the key to overcoming. The very first part of the word *submit* is *sub*. *Sub* means to place under, like a submarine places itself under water. When you place your life in submission to God, you are preparing yourself for victory.

> Therefore submit to God. Resist the devil and he will flee from you.
>
> —James 4:7

Notice the Bible says, "Submit to God," then, "Resist the devil," and finally, "he will flee." The very first step to breaking the power of iniquity and satanic influence is submission to God. It's in submission to God that we find the strength to resist the devil. When we submit to God, we no longer fight Satan alone, but God joins our struggle. Our God-dependent resistance is too much for the devil, and he has to flee.

So submit to God, wave the white flag of surrender, and resist the devil through the power of the Lord.

2. Claim the blood power over your life.

God will cancel the curse where the blood of Jesus is applied. Jesus is the once-and-for-all sacrifice, whose blood has given us victory over the curse of iniquity.

> Without shedding of blood there is no remission [of sin].
> —HEBREWS 9:22

The word *remission* is a very amazing word that means to dismiss or send away. If someone is battling cancer, what he or she most desires to hear is that the cancer is in remission. When someone receives a report that the cancer is in remission, it's a source of great celebration. What he or she is being told is this: "We have checked your body, blood, and bones, and we find no cancer. It is in remission." It has been dismissed and sent away.

When you claim the incredible power of the blood of Jesus, you experience victory. God looks at you, and because of the blood, He sees no sin in you whatsoever! Your sin has been dismissed and sent away.

The blood of Jesus puts sin in remission. Apply the blood to every single generational curse that would try to attach itself to your life. Jesus shed His blood so each curse of sin could be broken. The blood is an unstoppable weapon that places iniquitous, generational curse-producing sin in remission.

3. Forgive your family.

If you are wrestling with a generational curse, it is imperative that you walk in total forgiveness toward your family. Human tendency is to hold on to bitter, bondage-producing feelings, but you must not do it. Unforgiveness is toxic and will hinder you from living in the freedom and liberty that you so desperately need.

> And whenever you stand praying, if you have anything against anyone, forgive him, that your Father in heaven may also forgive you your trespasses.
> —MARK 11:25

There is great freedom in forgiveness. The person or persons you forgive may not even want or desire your forgiveness. Your forgiveness is not something they seek and will in no way set them free, but you must forgive them anyway.

Your forgiveness may not set them free, but your forgiveness will do something greater: it will set *you* free. Forgiveness is without a doubt one of the major steps to walking in freedom and liberty. In releasing those who failed before you, you are releasing yourself.

4. Confess your sin and the sin that was present in the generations before you.

> But if they confess their iniquity and the iniquity of their fathers, with their unfaithfulness in which they were unfaithful to Me, and that they also have walked contrary to Me...then I will remember My covenant.
> —LEVITICUS 26:40, 42

I am certainly not saying that the sin of our forefathers has any bearing on our eternal destiny. Certainly when we repent we are saved through the blood of Jesus Christ. We cannot be condemned by the behavior of the unrighteous acts of our forefathers any more than we can be saved by their righteous ones. As far as your salvation and eternal destiny are concerned, your sin is cleansed and you are saved when you confess Jesus as Lord.

In confessing the iniquity of those who have gone before you, you are acknowledging that this has been a stronghold in your family. This is an act of faith. As you do this, you are declaring that the drawing and tendency toward this sin that existed in your family will not exist in you. It is broken.

5. Use the powerful name of Jesus.

The powerful name of Jesus is accessible to you. Everything you need is received through His mighty name.

> And whatever you ask in My name, that I will do, that the Father may be glorified in the Son. If you ask anything in My name, I will do it.
> —JOHN 14:13–14

Ask in Jesus's name! Ask for freedom, deliverance, and total victory over every generational curse. There is no power in hell and no stronghold of sin that is greater than His mighty name. The Bible says in the Book of Philippians that Jesus has been given a name that is above every name (Phil. 2:9). Sickness, addiction, poverty, anger, or any other thing we can name is no match for the magnificent name of Jesus.

Every generational curse is broken through the authority of His mighty name! I have known people over the years who loved to drop names. In doing so, they were trying to let everyone know the powerful and influential people they knew. You know the most powerful man who ever lived; you know Jesus! It's time for you to start doing some *real* name dropping!

6. Break the curse by faith off those who will come after you.

Proverbs 18:21 declares that death and life are in the power of the tongue. Speak in faith and declare that the power of every generational curse is broken off your family.

I challenge you to pray this in faith. If there is a stronghold that I have not covered, add it to this prayer. There is no greater force available than the power of prayer. You may be thinking, "What if it doesn't work?" My reply would be: "What if it does?"

I confess and acknowledge my sin, and the sin of those who have gone before me. Their bondage shall not be mine, nor shall it be the generations' that will come after me. In the name of Jesus I break every generational curse off of my family and me.

Generational health problems, heart disease, cancer, diabetes, high blood pressure, glaucoma, arthritis, ulcers, breathing problems, blood disorders, bone degeneration, all hereditary sickness is broken in Jesus's name.

Eating disorders, overeating, anorexia, bulimia, or any type of eating that would destroy or harm our bodies is destroyed.

Alcoholism, addiction, and all sexual immorality is broken from my line.

Divorce, unforgiveness, addictions, depression, sorrow, gossip, worry, peer pressure, greed, bitterness, anger, temper, unworthiness, wounds, frustration, greed, compromise, smoking, and poverty—I declare all these broken in the name of Jesus and by His shed blood. My family and I walk in freedom and power, liberated from every generational curse for the glory of God. In Jesus's mighty name, amen!

7. Commit yourself to changing your behavior.

Make up your mind; there will be no behavior that you participate in that will in any way nurture satanic strongholds. If you have dealt with gossip, avoid those who listen. If you battled addiction, stay away from the people and places that could affect you. If you have had anger, sexual sin, or anything else, avoid connecting to the people, events, or places that act as triggers for those behaviors. Change your habits.

When you change your habits, you change your life.

8. Rejoice every day in knowing that God is faithful!

God is faithful. Rejoice in knowing that your life is free from the effects of generational curses. Claim in faith that this is a new beginning for you and those you love who are coming after you.

Feed your faith and starve your fear. Pray, read your Bible, and be faithful to a church where you can be taught the Word, build wholesome relationships, and grow in the Lord.

FOR A THOUSAND GENERATIONS

> Therefore know that the LORD your God, He is God, the faithful God who keeps covenant and mercy for a thousand generations with those who love Him and keep His commandments.
>
> —DEUTERONOMY 7:9

Joyfully confess that your family is blessed by a faithful God for a thousand generations!

Chapter 12

SPELL BREAKERS, ARISE

O N September 6, 2005, a beautiful baby boy was
born in a city hospital. He was born to a family known to
have intense and harsh struggles with addictions. In their own way
this family loved this little guy, but addictive behaviors are a heavy
weight to bear when trying to raise a baby.

Tiny ones born into this atmosphere often spend much time
neglected and alone. Parents of these children often roam the
streets trying to satisfy their habits. This precious little blue-eyed
baby probably understood this reality way too young. His bottle
was filled with Sprite as he stayed in his crib for hours on end. It
was said that as young as two years old, he would climb out of his
crib and crawl up the stairs of their crumbling apartment. An old
woman lived above him, and he would cry out for her to take care
of him and give him a little something to eat.

Early on there were frequent visitations by the police and exten-
sive arrests because of violence and trouble. Finally, after much
trouble, this little guy was removed from such a destructive and
deadly environment.

At three years old he rode in a car for the first time. It was the
police car that drove him away from the only home he ever knew.

When he arrived at the house of his foster parents, he was something to see. He was angry and disoriented. As he raged in fear,
he used the filthy language he had learned from the hard environment he had been raised in. He was skinny and pale, with teeth so

decayed and rotted by the sugary soda that he writhed in anguish every time he ate. He had to be put to sleep while almost all of his teeth underwent extreme dental work. His teeth were capped so he could begin to eat without pain.

He certainly had a harsh beginning and things seemed bleak, but his story wasn't over; it was only just starting. This was just a chapter in his book of life; it wasn't his whole story.

Never judge the book of your life based on one chapter; sometimes you need to turn the page and move on.

You see, the family that took him in that night was a family that loved Jesus. The love they had for Jesus caused them to love this little guy right through his issues. His foster parents put him in preschool and started bringing him to church. He made a lot of new friends, and because of the white caps, he had a million-dollar smile. He began to thrive rather than just survive. The foster mom had her eye on a family in the church she thought would be a great fit for him. In her own way she started trying to make this happen.

> Never judge the book of your life based on one chapter;
> sometimes you need to turn the page and move on.

The family she was eyeing already had a teenage daughter in middle school and an older daughter in college. They were happy, blessed, and shared a home filled with love, peace, and joy. It was just the place this fella needed, and he was just the guy to complete this family.

I personally know a lot about this adoptive family as well as this precious boy. That blue-eyed heart-stealer in now our son, and our girls have a little brother. The adoptive family is my family. We have a judge in our church who oversaw the process, and now it's official. Peyton James Raley got a new home, and Dawn and I got a new son.

ADOPTION CHANGES EVERYTHING

One of the most beautiful expressions of love in the world is found in the process of adoption. It is amazing to note that as children of God, each one of us has been adopted.

> But when the fullness of the time had come, God sent forth His Son, born of a woman, born under the law, to redeem those who were under the law, that we might receive the adoption as sons. And because you are sons, God has sent forth the Spirit of His Son into your hearts, crying out, "Abba, Father!" Therefore you are no longer a slave but a son, and if a son, then an heir of God through Christ.
>
> —GALATIANS 4:4–7

We are adopted. Even the word *adopt* is life transforming. The word *adopt* is actually made up of two words—*ad* and *opt*. Therefore, *adopt* means to opt to add. When we understand that, it makes what God did for us all the more awesome. Paul uses amazing imagery in the Book of Galatians concerning adoption. We must never forget we were an option. God didn't have to adopt us, but in love He opted to add us. Adoption is the highest blessing of the gospel.

We certainly don't view our son as an option, but the truth is, in the natural sense, he was. Our love for him caused us to make a place for him, and we chose him out of that great love.

> [Jesus said,] You did not choose Me, but I chose you.
>
> —JOHN 15:16

God loves you so intensely that He chose you. Maybe you have struggles, issues, and a whole lot of baggage. If that's your reality, you're still OK; that changes nothing. He loves you so much He adopted you anyway.

When we adopted our son, he got a brand-new birth certificate and even a new social security number. On his birth certificate I am listed as his father, and my wife is listed as his mother. His past has been completely erased.

In the eyes of the law my son is a brand-new person. In their eyes the connection he had to his old life is canceled; it's as if it never existed. He is seen as a brand-new boy.

When you were adopted into the family of God, your past was canceled, and now you are viewed as a brand-new creation in Christ Jesus. It doesn't matter what you did in your past or what has happened to you. As an adopted child of God you are cleared from all the guilt and shame of what was. You experience closeness, love, affection, and generosity straight from the heart of the Father.

In the Bible days, as well as today, there's an adoption price that often had to be paid. In ancient times the adoptive father was required to come up with that price. It was the only way he could adopt the child and claim him as his own. It is the same with us who have been adopted by our heavenly Father. He had to pay a great price.

> You were bought at a price.
> —1 CORINTHIANS 6:20

The adoption price paid for you and me was extreme to say the least. Our adoption price was the precious blood of Jesus Christ. Never give anyone the right to make you feel of no worth or value. You have been adopted, and a heavy price has been paid in order for you to experience the love of the Father. That price was the steepest price ever paid in all of human history so you could become a part of the family of God. Don't let anyone undervalue you and underestimate your worth. God thinks you're valuable and precious—and Jesus believes you were "to die for."

When we adopted our son, his name was changed. He now carries my name. He will perpetuate the Raley name, and it will live on through him. He has been grafted into my family. Every generational curse of his former family, from anger to addiction, has been broken off his life. He now lives as my son and has joined my daughters as my heir. The blessing of my home rests on him. He has my love, protection, and provision. I allow no harm to come his way, and I joyfully supply whatever he needs. I do so because he is my son, and I do it because I love him.

When he came into our home, he didn't quite know how to act at first. He really had no understanding of prayer. When he would say bedtime prayers, he didn't even know to say amen when he finished. He completed his prayers by saying, "in Jesus's name, the end!" But that just made us love him more.

He's six now, and he loves to play T-ball and football. He enjoys swimming, playing video games, and aggravating his sisters. His greatest joy? Going to church! He asks every day, "Is today church?" He's just as beautiful as he ever was, but he's not the same little guy. He knows he's loved, cared for, and protected. He knows who his father is, and he will ask me for anything.

You are a child of God, and you have been adopted to perpetuate His glorious name. You bear His name, and because you do, you're an heir. In fact, Jesus died so you could be heirs to the good things of the Father. All heaven has to offer is made available to you by your heavenly Father: salvation, healing, victory, provision, and breakthrough are yours as His precious child.

You have been adopted. He opted to add you because He loves you.

For this reason we should not fear Satan. He understands who you are in Christ and becomes very afraid when you grasp it. We established at the beginning of this book that Satan has risen to be the ultimate hater. But no matter how great his hate, hate doesn't conquer; love does. The power of the ultimate hater is overcome by the boundless love of the ultimate lover, Jesus Christ.

You are somebody special. You have been adopted, and you are loved! Adoption is so mighty when you recognize who you are. Powerful people were adopted in the Bible. Pharaoh's daughter adopted Moses, and Mordecai adopted Esther. Job cared for

unnamed orphans, and Joseph adopted Jesus. God through Jesus
Christ has adopted you, and you're in great company!

SPELL BREAKER, ARISE!

Don't allow yourself to walk in fear concerning any of hell's spells.
Push back against the enemy and remind him of who you are. You
are an heir, you walk by faith, and you are a part of God's family!

Realize who you are in Christ and that God is for you and He is
with you. Spell breaker, arise in the name of Jesus and declare that
there is not a spell birthed in hell that will ever overcome you! Your
destiny is victory!

In faith see yourself and your family walking in completeness
and joy. Wrap every ounce of faith in the love that God has for you
as His chosen child. Stop right now, rejoice in the Lord, and borrow
some praise from your future.

Spell breaker, the best is yet to come!

In Jesus's name, the end!

NOTES

CHAPTER 2
KNOW YOUR FOE

1. Billy Graham, *Angels* (Nashville: Thomas Nelson, 2011).

CHAPTER 3
THE FIGHT OF YOUR LIFE

1. BlueLetterBible.org, s.v. *"pale,"* http://www.blueletterbible.org/lang/lexicon/lexicon.cfm?Strongs=G3823&t=KJV (accessed June 1, 2012).

CHAPTER 5
THE CHARMED CHURCH

1. CoffeeFashion.com, "Decaffeination," http://coffee.gourmetrecipe.com/Decaffeination (accessed May 8, 2012).

CHAPTER 6
THE JEZEBEL SPIRIT

1. Dictionary.com, *Dictionary.com Unabridged*, Random House, Inc., s.v. "tolerate," http://dictionary.reference.com/cite.html?qh=tolerate&ia=luna (accessed May 8, 2012).

CHAPTER 7
A SMILING REBELLION

1. *Merriam-Webster's Collegiate Dictionary*, 11th ed. (Springfield, MA: Merriam-Webster, Inc., 2003), s.v. "oppress."

FREE NEWSLETTERS
TO HELP EMPOWER YOUR LIFE

Why subscribe today?

❑ **DELIVERED DIRECTLY TO YOU.** All you have to do is open your inbox and read.

❑ **EXCLUSIVE CONTENT.** We cover the news overlooked by the mainstream press.

❑ **STAY CURRENT.** Find the latest court rulings, revivals, and cultural trends.

❑ **UPDATE OTHERS.** Easy to forward to friends and family with the click of your mouse.

CHOOSE THE E-NEWSLETTER THAT INTERESTS YOU MOST:

- Christian news
- Daily devotionals
- Spiritual empowerment
- And much, much more

SIGN UP AT: **http://freenewsletters.charismamag.com**

8178